Apache Mesos Cookb

Powerful recipes and useful techniques to get started with
Apache Mesos

David Blomquist
Tomasz Janiszewski

BIRMINGHAM - MUMBAI

Apache Mesos Cookbook

First published: July 2017

Production reference: 1310717

Published by Packt Publishing Ltd.
Livery Place
35 Livery Street
Birmingham
B3 2PB, UK.

ISBN 978-1-78588-462-7

www.packtpub.com

Credits

Authors
David Blomquist
Tomasz Janiszewski

Reviewer
Radoslaw Gruchalski

Commissioning Editor
Kunal Parikh

Acquisition Editor
Meeta Rajani

Content Development Editor
Mamata Walkar

Technical Editor
Varsha Shivhare

Copy Editor
Safis Editing

Project Coordinator
Kinjal Bari

Proofreader
Safis Editing

Indexer
Pratik Shirodkar

Graphics
Kirk D'penha

Production Coordinator
Shantanu Zagade

About the Authors

David Blomquist has worked with computer technology for almost 30 years. He studied electrical engineering at Arizona State University and chemical engineering at the University of Texas. David is currently the president and CTO of Tentra, a systems integration company. When he is not wrangling large-scale container deployments into well behaved PaaS herds, he can be found skiing; or hiking, while patiently waiting for the next ski season to begin.

Tomasz Janiszewski is a software engineer who is passionate about distributed systems. He believes in free and open source philosophy and occasionally contributes to projects on GitHub. He actively participates in the Mesos community and spreads his knowledge on mailing lists and StackOverflow. He is involved in Marathon development and building PaaS on top of Mesos and Marathon.

About the Reviewer

Radoslaw Gruchalski is a software engineer specializing in distributed systems. With over 17 years' commercial experience, 5 of which have been exclusively in the IoT and big data processing landscape, he currently focuses on helping his clients in the area of design, architecture, and the implementation of distributed, fault-tolerant platforms for cloud, hybrid, and on-premise deployments. His hands-on experience with the design, architectural, implementation, and operational aspects of the SMACK stack, together with his deep understanding of what it takes to deploy distributed systems, makes him an invaluable asset to have in your team.

www.PacktPub.com

For support files and downloads related to your book, please visit www.PacktPub.com. Did you know that Packt offers eBook versions of every book published, with PDF and ePub files available? You can upgrade to the eBook version at www.PacktPub.com and as a print book customer, you are entitled to a discount on the eBook copy. Get in touch with us at service@packtpub.com for more details. At www.PacktPub.com, you can also read a collection of free technical articles, sign up for a range of free newsletters and receive exclusive discounts and offers on Packt books and eBooks.

https://www.packtpub.com/mapt

Get the most in-demand software skills with Mapt. Mapt gives you full access to all Packt books and video courses, as well as industry-leading tools to help you plan your personal development and advance your career.

Why subscribe?

- Fully searchable across every book published by Packt
- Copy and paste, print, and bookmark content
- On demand and accessible via a web browser

Customer Feedback

Thanks for purchasing this Packt book. At Packt, quality is at the heart of our editorial process. To help us improve, please leave us an honest review on this book's Amazon page at `https://www.amazon.com/dp/178588462X`.

If you'd like to join our team of regular reviewers, you can email us at `customerreviews@packtpub.com`. We award our regular reviewers with free eBooks and videos in exchange for their valuable feedback. Help us be relentless in improving our products!

Table of Contents

Chapter 5: Managing Containers

Preface

Apache Mesos was the first open source cluster manager to handle workloads in a distributed environment through dynamic resource sharing and isolation. It is great for deploying and managing applications in large-scale cluster environments.

Since its inception, Mesos has been under constant development and it is one of the most mature, robust and stable cluster managers in both the open source and commercial software worlds.

This guide is packed with powerful recipes for using Apache Mesos and its integration with containers and frameworks.

What this book covers

Chapter 1, *Getting Started with Apache Mesos*, provides instructions for installing Mesos on several different operating systems.

Chapter 2, *Implementing High Availability with Apache ZooKeeper*, teaches you how to install Apache Zookeeper and configure it with Mesos to create a multi-master, highly available Mesos cluster.

Chapter 3, *Running and Maintaining Mesos*, describes the components of a running Mesos cluster and shows you how to configure them.

Chapter 4, *Understanding the Scheduler API*, first teaches you about frameworks and how they interact with Mesos, then proceeds to show you how to develop a simple framework.

Chapter 5, *Managing Containers*, shows you how to deploy and manage containerizers in Mesos.

Chapter 6, *Deploying PaaS with Marathon*, demonstrates how to install and configure Marathon and other tools required to set up a private PaaS.

Chapter 7, *Job Scheduling with Metronome*, shows you how to run a cron service on Mesos.

Chapter 8, *Continuous Integration with Jenkins*, teaches you how to run a highly scalable Jenkins continuous integration and continuous delivery system on Mesos.

What you need for this book

We recommend one server or virtual machine installed with Ubuntu 14.04 as a development environment for following most of the recipes in this book. To test the high availability recipes in Chapter 2, *Implementing High Availability with Apache ZooKeeper* a minimum of six servers or virtual machines is required. Chapters 1, *Getting Started with Apache Mesos* and Chapter 2, *Implementing High Availability with Apache ZooKeeper* will guide you through installing and configuring Mesos and ZooKeeper on multiple operating systems but we recommend mastering the recipes in chapters 3 – 8 on Ubuntu 14.04 before adapting them for other supported operating systems.

Who this book is for

This book is for systems administrators, engineers, and programmers who are interested in using Mesos. Basic experience with distributed systems and cluster management would be helpful but is not essential. A working knowledge of the Linux operating system is expected.

Sections

In this book, you will find several headings that appear frequently (Getting ready, How to do it…, How it works…, There's more…, and See also). To give clear instructions on how to complete a recipe, we use these sections as follows:

Getting ready

This section tells you what to expect in the recipe, and describes how to set up any software or any preliminary settings required for the recipe.

How to do it…

This section contains the steps required to follow the recipe.

How it works…

This section usually consists of a detailed explanation of what happened in the previous section.

There's more...

This section consists of additional information about the recipe in order to make the reader more knowledgeable about the recipe.

See also

This section provides helpful links to other useful information for the recipe.

Conventions

In this book, you will find a number of text styles that distinguish between different kinds of information. Here are some examples of these styles and an explanation of their meaning.

Code words in text, database table names, folder names, filenames, file extensions, pathnames, dummy URLs, user input, and Twitter handles are shown as follows: " By default, Marathon logs to stdout and syslog."

A block of code is set as follows:

```
cat <<EOF > /etc/systemd/system/traefik.service
[Unit]
Description=Traefik
Wants=network-online.target
After=network.target network-online.target
[Service]
Restart=on-failure
ExecStart=/usr/bin/traefik
[Install]
WantedBy=multi-user.target
EOF
```

Any command-line input or output is written as follows:

```
curl -k https://localhost:8443/ping
```

New terms and **important words** are shown in bold. Words that you see on the screen, for example, in menus or dialog boxes, appear in the text like this: " You should also be able to see Marathon listed as a framework in the **Mesos UI Frameworks** tab."

Warnings or important notes appear like this.

 Tips and tricks appear like this.

Reader feedback

Feedback from our readers is always welcome. Let us know what you think about this book-what you liked or disliked. Reader feedback is important for us as it helps us develop titles that you will really get the most out of. To send us general feedback, simply email feedback@packtpub.com, and mention the book's title in the subject of your message. If there is a topic that you have expertise in and you are interested in either writing or contributing to a book, see our author guide at www.packtpub.com/authors.

Customer support

Now that you are the proud owner of a Packt book, we have a number of things to help you to get the most from your purchase.

Downloading the example code

You can download the example code files for this book from your account at http://www.packtpub.com. If you purchased this book elsewhere, you can visit http://www.packtpub.com/support and register to have the files emailed directly to you. You can download the code files by following these steps:

1. Log in or register to our website using your email address and password.
2. Hover the mouse pointer on the **SUPPORT** tab at the top.
3. Click on **Code Downloads & Errata**.
4. Enter the name of the book in the **Search** box.
5. Select the book for which you're looking to download the code files.
6. Choose from the drop-down menu where you purchased this book from.
7. Click on **Code Download**.

You can also download the code files by clicking on the **Code Files** button on the book's webpage at the Packt Publishing website. This page can be accessed by entering the book's name in the **Search** box. Please note that you need to be logged in to your Packt account. Once the file is downloaded, please make sure that you unzip or extract the folder using the latest version of:

- WinRAR / 7-Zip for Windows
- Zipeg / iZip / UnRarX for Mac
- 7-Zip / PeaZip for Linux

The code bundle for the book is also hosted on GitHub at `https://github.com/PacktPublishing/Apache-Mesos-Cookbook`. We also have other code bundles from our rich catalog of books and videos available at `https://github.com/PacktPublishing/`. Check them out!

Downloading the color images of this book

We also provide you with a PDF file that has color images of the screenshots/diagrams used in this book. The color images will help you better understand the changes in the output. You can download this file from `https://www.packtpub.com/sites/default/files/downloads/ApacheMesosCookbook_ColorImages.pdf`.

Errata

Although we have taken every care to ensure the accuracy of our content, mistakes do happen. If you find a mistake in one of our books-maybe a mistake in the text or the code-we would be grateful if you could report this to us. By doing so, you can save other readers from frustration and help us improve subsequent versions of this book. If you find any errata, please report them by visiting `http://www.packtpub.com/submit-errata`, selecting your book, clicking on the **Errata Submission Form** link, and entering the details of your errata. Once your errata are verified, your submission will be accepted and the errata will be uploaded to our website or added to any list of existing errata under the Errata section of that title. To view the previously submitted errata, go to `https://www.packtpub.com/books/content/support` and enter the name of the book in the search field. The required information will appear under the **Errata** section.

Piracy

Piracy of copyrighted material on the internet is an ongoing problem across all media. At Packt, we take the protection of our copyright and licenses very seriously. If you come across any illegal copies of our works in any form on the internet, please provide us with the location address or website name immediately so that we can pursue a remedy. Please contact us at copyright@packtpub.com with a link to the suspected pirated material. We appreciate your help in protecting our authors and our ability to bring you valuable content.

Questions

If you have a problem with any aspect of this book, you can contact us at questions@packtpub.com, and we will do our best to address the problem.

1
Getting Started with Apache Mesos

In this chapter, we present an overview of the Mesos architecture and recipes for installing Mesos on Linux and Mac. The following are the recipes covered in this chapter:

- Installing Mesos on Ubuntu 16.04 from packages
- Installing Mesos on Ubuntu 14.04 from packages
- Installing Mesos on CentOS 7 and RHEL 7 from packages
- Preparing Ubuntu 16.04 for a Mesos installation from source code
- Preparing Ubuntu 14.04 for a Mesos installation from source code
- Preparing OS X (Yosemite and El Capitan) for a Mesos installation from source code
- Downloading, building, and installing the Mesos source code

Introduction

Apache Mesos is cluster management software that distributes the combined resources of many individual servers to applications through frameworks. Mesos is open source software that is free to download and use in accordance with the Apache License 2.0. This chapter will provide the reader with recipes for installing and configuring Apache Mesos.

Mesos can run on Linux, Mac, and Windows. However, we recommend running Mesos on Linux for production deployments and on Mac and Windows for development purposes only. Mesos can be installed from source code or from binary packages downloaded from repositories. We will cover a few installation methods on select operating systems in this chapter. The reasons for covering these specific operating systems and installation methods are as follows:

- The operating systems natively include a kernel that supports full resource isolation
- The operating systems are current as of this writing with long-term support
- The operating systems and installation methods do not require workarounds or an excessive number of external repositories
- The installation methods use the latest stable version of Mesos, whether it is from binary packages or source code

Based on these criteria, we have covered the following installation methods for this book:

- Mesosphere packages on Ubuntu 16.04 LTS
- Mesosphere packages on Ubuntu 14.04 LTS
- Mesosphere packages on CentOS 7 and RHEL 7
- Source code on Ubuntu 16.04 LTS
- Source code on Ubuntu 14.04 LTS
- Source code on OS X (Yosemite and El Capitan)

Mesosphere, a company founded by one of the original developers of Mesos, provides free, open source binary packages as well as commercial support for Mesos. Mesosphere binary packages are well maintained and provide an easy way to install and run Mesos. We use Mesosphere packages installed on Ubuntu 14.04 as the base environment for the recipes in chapters 3 – 8 and we recommend you use that installation method with this book. If you need to run Mesos one of the other supported operating systems, we provide you with the installation instructions in this chapter but you will need to adapt the recipes in chapters 3 – 8 for use with your operating system. Installing Mesos from source will allow you to customize the build and install process and enable and disable features so we will also guide you through a source install in this chapter. If you want a development environment on a Mac, building from source on OS X is the only way to go.

We will guide you through the installations in the following sections but first, you will need to plan your Mesos deployment. For a Mesos development environment, you only need one host or node. The node can be a physical computer, a virtual machine, or a cloud instance. For a production cluster, we recommend at least three master nodes and as many slave nodes as you will need to support your application frameworks. You can think of the slave nodes as a pool of CPU, RAM, and storage that can be increased by simply adding more slave nodes. Mesos makes it very easy to add slave nodes to an existing cluster as your application requirements grow. At this point, you should determine whether you will be building a Mesos development environment or a production cluster and you should have an idea of how many master and slave nodes you will need. The next sections will provide recipes for installing Mesos in the environment of your choice.

Installing Mesos on Ubuntu 16.04 from packages

In this recipe, we will be installing Mesos `.deb` packages from the Mesosphere repositories using `apt`.

Getting ready

You must be running a 64-bit version of the Ubuntu 16.04 operating system and it should be patched to the most current patch level using `apt-get` prior to installing the Mesos packages.

How to do it...

1. First, download and install the OpenPGP key for the Mesosphere packages:

   ```
   $ sudo apt-key adv --keyserver keyserver.ubuntu.com --recv
   E56151BF
   ```

2. Now install the Mesosphere repository:

   ```
   $ DISTRO=$(lsb_release -is | tr '[:upper:]' '[:lower:]')
   $ CODENAME=$(lsb_release -cs)
   $ echo "deb http://repos.mesosphere.io/${DISTRO} ${CODENAME}
   main"|
   sudo tee /etc/apt/sources.list.d/mesosphere.list
   ```

3. Update the `apt-get` package indexes:

```
$ sudo apt-get update
```

4. Install Mesos and the included ZooKeeper binaries:

```
$ sudo apt-get -y install mesos
```

5. At this point, you can start Mesos to do some basic testing. To start the Mesos master and agent (slave) daemons, execute the following:

```
$ sudo service mesos-master start
$ sudo service mesos-slave start
```

6. To validate the Mesos installation, open a browser and point it to `http://<ipaddress>:5050`. Replace `<ipaddress>` with the actual address of the host with the new Mesos installation.

How it works...

The Mesosphere packages provide the software required to run Mesos. Next, you will configure ZooKeeper, which is covered in `Chapter 2`, *Implementing High Availability with Apache ZooKeeper*.

See also

If you prefer to build and install Mesos on Ubuntu from source code, we will cover that in an upcoming section in this chapter.

Installing Mesos on Ubuntu 14.04 from packages

In this recipe, we will be installing Mesos `.deb` packages from the Mesosphere repositories using `apt`.

Getting ready

You must be running a 64-bit version of the Ubuntu 14.04 operating system and it should be patched to the most current patch level using `apt-get` prior to installing the Mesos packages.

How to do it...

1. First, download and install the OpenPGP key for the Mesosphere packages:

   ```
   $ sudo apt-key adv --keyserver keyserver.ubuntu.com --recv
   E56151BF
   ```

2. Now install the Mesosphere repository:

   ```
   $ DISTRO=$(lsb_release -is | tr '[:upper:]' '[:lower:]')
   $ CODENAME=$(lsb_release -cs)
   $ echo "deb http://repos.mesosphere.io/${DISTRO} ${CODENAME} main"|
   sudo tee /etc/apt/sources.list.d/mesosphere.list
   ```

3. Update the `apt-get` package indexes:

   ```
   $ sudo apt-get update
   ```

4. Install Mesos and the included ZooKeeper binaries:

   ```
   $ sudo apt-get -y install mesos
   ```

5. At this point, you can start Mesos to do some basic testing. To start the Mesos master and agent (slave) daemons, execute the following command:

   ```
   $ sudo service mesos-master start
   $ sudo service mesos-slave start
   ```

6. To validate the Mesos installation, open a browser and point it to `http://<ipaddress>:5050`. Replace `<ipaddress>` with the actual address of the host with the new Mesos installation.

How it works...

The Mesosphere packages provide the software required to run Mesos. Next, you will configure ZooKeeper, which is covered in `Chapter 2`, *Implementing High Availability with Apache ZooKeeper*.

See also

If you prefer to build and install Mesos on Ubuntu from source code, we will cover that in an upcoming section in this chapter.

Installing Mesos on CentOS 7 and RHEL 7 from packages

In this recipe, we will be installing Mesos `.rpm` packages from the Mesosphere repositories using `yum`.

Getting ready

Your CentOS 7 or RHEL 7 operating system should be patched to the most current patch level using `yum` prior to installing the Mesosphere packages.

How to do it...

1. First, add the Mesosphere repository:

   ```
   $ sudo rpm -Uvh
   http://repos.mesosphere.io/el/7/noarch/RPMS/mesosphere-el-repo-
   7-1.noarch.rpm
   ```

2. And now, install Mesos and ZooKeeper:

   ```
   $ sudo yum -y install mesos mesosphere-zookeeper
   ```

3. At this point, you can start Mesos to do some basic testing. To start the Mesos master and agent (slave) daemons, execute the following:

```
$ sudo service mesos-master start
$ sudo service mesos-slave start
```

4. To validate the Mesos installation, open a browser and point it to `http://<ipaddress>:5050`. Replace `<ipaddress>` with the actual address of the host with the new Mesos installation.

How it works...

The Mesosphere packages provide the software required to run Mesos. Next, you will configure ZooKeeper, which is covered in `Chapter 2`, *Implementing High Availability with Apache ZooKeeper*.

See also

If you prefer to build and install Mesos from source code on RHEL 7 or CentOS 7, you can find installation instructions for CentOS 7 on the `mesos.apache.org` website. We do not cover installing Mesos source code on RHEL7 or CentOS 7 in this book due to dependencies that require packages from multiple third-party repositories.

Preparing Ubuntu 16.04 for a Mesos installation from source code

In this recipe, we will prepare the Ubuntu 16.04 operating system for a Mesos source code installation.

Getting ready

You must be running a 64-bit version of the Ubuntu 16.04 operating system and it should be patched to the most current patch level using `apt-get` prior to building the Mesos source code.

How to do it...

1. First, we need to sync the latest package lists from the apt repositories with the update command:

   ```
   $ sudo apt-get update
   ```

2. Then we will install the prerequisite packages for building and running the Mesos source code:

   ```
   $ sudo apt-get install -y tar wget git openjdk-8-
   jdk autoconf libtool
   build-essential python-dev python-boto libcurl4-
   nss-dev libsasl2-dev
   libsasl2-modules maven libapr1-dev libsvn-dev
   libghc-zlib-dev
   ```

3. Next, continue to the *Downloading, building, and installing the Mesos source code* recipe at the end of this chapter.

How it works...

Preparing the operating system will enable us to build and install the Mesos source code. Next, you will need to download the Mesos source files and build the code.

Preparing Ubuntu 14.04 for a Mesos installation from source code

In this recipe, we will prepare the Ubuntu 14.04 operating system for a Mesos source code installation.

Getting ready

You must be running a 64-bit version of the Ubuntu 14.04 operating system and it should be patched to the most current patch level using apt-get prior to building the Mesos source code.

How to do it...

1. First, we need to sync the latest package lists from the apt repositories with the update command:

   ```
   $ sudo apt-get update
   ```

2. Then, we install the prerequisite packages for building and running the Mesos source code:

   ```
   $ sudo apt-get install -y tar wget git openjdk-7-
   jdk autoconf libtool
   build-essential python-dev python-boto libcurl4-
   nss-dev libsasl2-dev
   libsasl2-modules maven libapr1-dev libsvn-dev
   ```

3. Next, continue to the *Downloading, building, and installing the Mesos source code* recipe at the end of this chapter.

How it works...

Preparing the operating system will enable us to build and install the Mesos source code. Next, you will need to download the Mesos source files and build the code.

Preparing OS X (Yosemite and El Capitan) for a Mesos Installation from source code

In this recipe, we will prepare the OS X operating system for a Mesos source code installation.

Getting ready

Building the current version of Mesos (which is 1.0.1 at the time of this writing) requires GCC 4.8.1+ or Clang 3.5+. You should be running a 64-bit version of OS X and it should be patched to the most current patch level prior to building the Mesos source code.

How to do it...

1. Install command-line tools, Homebrew, Java, and libraries required for Mesos:

```
$ xcode-select --install
$ ruby -e "$(curl -fsSL
https://raw.githubusercontent.com/Homebrew/install/master/insta
ll)"
$ brew install Caskroom/cask/java
$ brew install wget git autoconf automake libtool subversion
maven
```

2. Next, continue to the *Downloading, building, and installing the Mesos source code* recipe at the end of this chapter.

How it works...

Preparing the operating system will enable us to build and install the Mesos source code. Next, you will need to download the Mesos source files and build the code.

Downloading, building, and installing the Mesos source code

In this recipe, we will download the Mesos source files, build the code, and install the Mesos binaries and libraries.

Getting ready

Follow the previous sections in this chapter to prepare your operating system for a Mesos source installation.

How to do it...

1. Browse to the following location: `http://mesos.apache.org/downloads/`.

2. Download the TAR file for the most recent stable release of Mesos. For example, to download Mesos version 1.0.1:

   ```
   $ wget http://www.apache.org/dist/mesos/1.0.1/mesos-1.0.1.tar.gz
   ```

3. Extract the contents of the TAR file. For example, to extract the Mesos 1.0.1 TAR file:

   ```
   $ tar xvzf mesos-1.0.1.tar.gz
   ```

4. Change the directory to the extracted TAR file directory created in the previous step, for example:

   ```
   $ cd mesos-1.0.1
   ```

5. Create the `build` directory:

   ```
   $ mkdir build
   ```

6. Change directory to the `build` directory:

   ```
   $ cd build
   ```

7. Configure the Mesos build script. You can run `../configure --help` to see all the available configuration options. Refer to the *There's more...* section at the end of this recipe for more configuration tips:

   ```
   $ ../configure
   ```

8. Build the Mesos binaries (executing `'make -j <number of cores> V=0` will decrease both the build time and log verbosity on multicore systems). Refer to the *There's more...* section at the end of this recipe for more build tips:

   ```
   $ make
   ```

9. **Optional**: Run some tests:

   ```
   $ make check
   ```

10. **Optional**: Execute the `make install` command if you would like to install the Mesos binaries and libraries in `/usr/local/` and add them to the system path. Mesos can also be installed in other locations or run directly from the build directory. Refer to the *There's more...* section at the end of this recipe for instructions on installing Mesos to alternative locations, as well as for other installation tips:

    ```
    $ sudo make install
    ```

11. **Optional**: For Ubuntu only, create links to the Mesos libraries if you chose the default installation to `/usr/local`:

    ```
    $ sudo ldconfig
    ```

12. At this point, you can start Mesos to do some basic testing. To start the Mesos master and agent daemons, first create the `mesos` working directory:

    ```
    $ sudo mkdir /var/lib/mesos
    ```

13. Change into the Mesos source `build` directory:

    ```
    $ cd build
    ```

14. Now start the Mesos master:

    ```
    $ sudo ./bin/mesos-master.sh --ip=127.0.0.1 --
    work_dir=/var/lib/mesos
    ```

15. And start the Mesos agent (in a separate terminal session):

    ```
    $ sudo ./bin/mesos-agent.sh --master=127.0.0.1:5050 --
    work_dir=/var/lib/mesos
    ```

16. To validate the Mesos installation, open a browser on the Mesos host and point it to `http://127.0.0.1:5050`. If you wish to validate with a browser remotely, you will need to replace 127.0.0.1 with the real IP of the Mesos host in the previous commands and restart both the master and agent. You will also need to use the real IP of the Mesos host in the browser.

Warning

When using the real IP in the command line, the Mesos master and agent processes will fail to start unless the Mesos host is registered in DNS.

How it works...

Building the Mesos source code will create the binaries needed to run Mesos. Next, you will configure ZooKeeper, which is covered in `Chapter 2`, *Implementing High Availability with Apache ZooKeeper*.

There's more...

Refer to the following tips.

Configuration tips

There are a number of options that can be configured in the Mesos build script. For example, if you want to build Mesos with SSL support, you will need to enable the `ssl` and `libevent` features by executing `../configure --enable-ssl --enable-libevent` prior to executing `make`. To see a full list of the configure options, execute `../configure --help` from the Mesos `build` directory.

Build tips

If you are building out a Mesos cluster using hosts with the same operating system version, you can configure and build the source code on one server and then copy that source directory to the other servers. You can then skip the `../configure` and `make` commands and just run Mesos from the `build` directory or execute make install to install it without having to go through the build (`make`) process on every server.

If you do plan on copying pre-built Mesos software to other servers, make sure all of the servers have the supporting packages required to run Mesos and that the OS is patched to the same version.

Installation tips

The default behavior of `make install` is to install the Mesos binaries and libraries in the `/usr/local` path. If you would like to change the installation path, execute `../configure --prefix=/path/to/install/directory` during the configure stage prior to the build (`make`) and install (`make install`) stages.

If at some point you would like to uninstall the Mesos binaries from the installation path, you can execute `make uninstall` from the source code `build` directory. After building and installing the Mesos source code, we recommend archiving the source code directory for future reference.

2

Implementing High Availability with Apache ZooKeeper

In this chapter, you will learn to how to configure Apache ZooKeeper with Mesos and run a highly available cluster:

- Configuring ZooKeeper installed from packages
- Configuring ZooKeeper installed from source
- Running a standalone Mesos master with ZooKeeper
- Running a high-availability Mesos cluster with ZooKeeper

Introduction

Apache ZooKeeper is a distributed key-value store that provides centralized coordination, synchronization, naming, and group services for distributed systems. ZooKeeper was developed as an independent system that can be integrated with other large distributed systems so that developers can focus on distributed application development and not on coordination services. Mesos depends on ZooKeeper for leader election so configuring Mesos with ZooKeeper is critical to running a highly available Mesos cluster. We will guide you through installing ZooKeeper and then configuring it with Mesos.

In the following recipes, we will give examples for configuring both a single development Mesos instance with ZooKeeper and for a highly available, multi-master Mesos cluster with ZooKeeper. ZooKeeper is not required to run a single instance of Mesos. However, you may need to deploy a single instance of ZooKeeper with a single Mesos instance to support development of frameworks that depend on ZooKeeper. For production, you will need a minimum of three, and always an odd number, of ZooKeeper/Mesos master nodes to deploy a highly available cluster. The number of agents can be odd or even and the actual number of agents that you need will depend on the resources you require for your application. If you deploy Mesos with ZooKeeper, you will also need to choose the quorum value for your cluster. The general rule of thumb for assigning the quorum value is $(N+1)/2=quorum$ with N being the number of ZooKeeper/Mesos master nodes. For a single development instance, $N=1$ so our quorum value is $(1+1)/2=1$. For a cluster with three ZooKeeper/Mesos masters, our quorum value is $(3+1)/2=2$, and so on.

Configuring ZooKeeper installed from packages on Ubuntu 14.04, Ubuntu 16.04, CentOS 7, or RHEL 7

Getting ready

Please follow the instructions in `Chapter 1`, *Getting Started with Apache Mesos* for installing the Mesos packages from the Mesosphere repositories for your operating system prior to executing the following steps. ZooKeeper will be installed during the Mesos package installation. For a multi-master Mesos/ZooKeeper configuration, confirm that DNS A (host) and PTR (reverse lookup) records have been added to your DNS servers for your Mesos hosts.

How to do it...

This recipe will work for both the Ubuntu and CentOS operating systems but we will use the following configuration on 10 CentOS 7 VMs for our demo cluster:

Function	IP address	Hostname	Cluster	myid	Quorum
Master	10.10.0.70	centos7070	MesosCentOS7	70	2
Master	10.10.0.71	centos7071	MesosCentOS7	71	2

Master	10.10.0.72	centos7072	MesosCentOS7	72	2
Agent	10.10.0.73	centos7073	N/A	N/A	N/A
Agent	10.10.0.74	centos7074	N/A	N/A	N/A
Agent	10.10.0.75	centos7075	N/A	N/A	N/A
Agent	10.10.0.76	centos7076	N/A	N/A	N/A
Agent	10.10.0.77	centos7077	N/A	N/A	N/A
Agent	10.10.0.78	centos7078	N/A	N/A	N/A
Agent	10.10.0.79	centos7079	N/A	N/A	N/A

Configuring Mesos masters with ZooKeeper

1. Edit /var/lib/zookeeper/myid and replace all of the text in the file with a unique integer between 1 and 255. If you plan on building a multi-master Mesos cluster, the integer in this file is arbitrary but it will need to be unique for each ZooKeeper instance on each Mesos master server.

2. Edit /etc/zookeeper/conf/zoo.cfg and add a line similar to the following examples for each ZooKeeper instance in your Mesos cluster. The integer that comes after server must match the integers in the myid files created in *step 1* for each ZooKeeper instance in your cluster. The following are examples for both single server and multi-master Mesos clusters:

   - **Example 1**: This configuration is for a single ZooKeeper instance on a Mesos development machine so you would only need one line with the loopback address. The myid file (*step 1*) on this development machine would contain the integer 1:

     server.1=127.0.0.1:2888:3888

   - **Example 2**: This configuration is for a Mesos production cluster with three Mesos/ZooKeeper masters. Each master node is running a ZooKeeper instance with a unique integer in the myid file. The numbers after the server entries must match the integers in the myid files for the three ZooKeeper servers. The three ZooKeeper servers in this example have myid file entries of 1, 2, and 3 respectively. Replace the IP address (10.10.0.x) in the following examples with the real IP addresses of your Mesos masters:

     server.1=10.0.0.11:2888:3888
     server.2=10.0.0.32:2888:3888

```
server.3=10.0.0.25:2888:3888
```

3. Edit the `'dataDir='` setting in `/etc/zookeeper/conf/zoo.cfg` and set it to the directory where you want to store the ZooKeeper snapshot.

4. Edit `/etc/mesos/zk` and modify the default URL to match the IP address of the ZooKeeper/Mesos masters. For standalone Mesos instances, the default `url` may be left as is. The `url` for the Mesos production cluster example in *step 2* would look like this:

```
zk://10.0.0.11:2181,10.0.0.32:2181,10.0.0.25:2181/mesos
```

5. Edit `/etc/mesos-master/quorum` and modify the setting to an integer that is equal to more than half of the Mesos masters but no more than the total number of masters. For a standalone instance, this would be 1. For a production cluster, you generally would not want to include all of the Mesos masters in the quorum so that the cluster will still continue to operate if one master is down. For our three-node Mesos master example, the best setting is 2.

6. Create IP, hostname, and cluster files for each of the Mesos masters, changing the IP and hostname values for each master. The cluster name is arbitrary and can be whatever you would like to call your cluster but it must be the same for all masters:

```
$ echo "10.10.0.71" | sudo tee /etc/mesos-master/ip
$ echo "centos7071" | sudo tee /etc/mesos-
  master/hostname
$ echo "MesosCentOS7" | sudo tee /etc/mesos-
master/cluster
```

7. Restart ZooKeeper and the Mesos masters:

   - **Ubuntu 14.04**:

     ```
     $ sudo service zookeeper restart
     $ sudo service mesos-master restart
     ```

   - **CentOS7/RHEL7/Ubuntu 16.04**:

     ```
     $ sudo systemctl restart zookeeper
     $ sudo systemctl restart mesos-master
     ```

8. Disable Mesos agent (slave) services. If you are configuring a production Mesos cluster, you will want to run the Mesos masters on dedicated servers with the Mesos agent (slave) services disabled:

- **Ubuntu 14.04**:

```
$ sudo service mesos-slave stop
$ echo manual | sudo tee /etc/init/mesos-slave.override
```

- **CentOS7/RHEL7/Ubuntu 16.04**:

  - ```
    $ sudo systemctl stop mesos-slave
    $ sudo systemctl disable mesos-slave
    ```

9. Repeat *steps 1-8* on each Mesos master.

10. Once all of the Mesos masters are running, validate your cluster by pointing your browser to port `5050` on any of the master servers. Mesos masters running with ZooKeeper will only have one elected leader at a time. You can see which master is currently the leader by looking at the value for `Server:` in the upper-right corner of the Mesos UI:

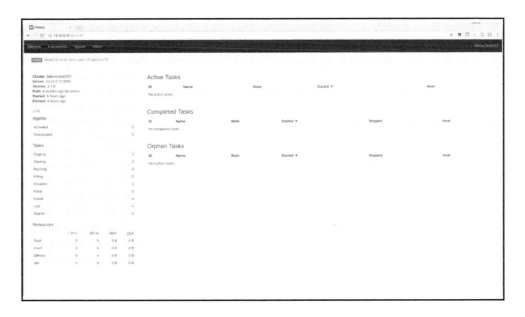
    ```

Configuring Mesos agents with ZooKeeper

1. Edit `/etc/mesos/zk` and add the same line that we used on the Mesos masters on all the Mesos agents. Edit as appropriate using the IP addresses of your Mesos masters. Using our example configuration from earlier:

```
$ echo
'zk://10.0.0.11:2181,10.0.0.32:2181,10.0.0.25:2181/mesos' |
sudo tee /etc/mesos/zk
```

2. Create IP and hostname files for each of the Mesos agents (slaves), changing the values for IP and hostname on each agent server:

```
$ echo "10.10.0.73" | sudo tee /etc/mesos-slave/ip
$ echo "ubuntu7073" | sudo tee /etc/mesos-slave/hostname
```

3. Disable ZooKeeper and Mesos master services:

   - **Ubuntu 14.04**:

     ```
     $ sudo service mesos-master stop
     $ echo manual | sudo tee /etc/init/mesos-
     master.override
     $ sudo service zookeeper stop
     $ echo manual | sudo tee /etc/init/zookeeper.override
     ```

   - **CentOS7/RHEL7/Ubuntu 16.04**:

     ```
     $ sudo systemctl stop mesos-master
     $ sudo systemctl disable mesos-master
     $ sudo systemctl stop zookeeper
     $ sudo systemctl disable zookeeper
     ```

4. Start or restart Mesos agents:

   - **Ubuntu 14.04**:

     ```
     $ sudo service mesos-slave restart
     ```

   - **CentOS7/RHEL7/Ubuntu 16.04**:

     ```
     $ sudo systemctl restart mesos-slave
     ```

5. Repeat *steps 1-4* on each Mesos agent server.
6. Validate that the agents are registered with the cluster by again pointing your browser to port 5050 on any one of the master servers. Then click on the **Agents** tab on the bar at the top of the Mesos UI. You should see the newly registered agents:

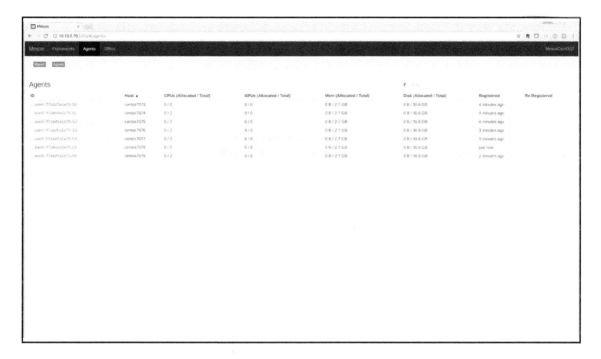

How it works...

Configuring Mesos with ZooKeeper will allow you to run a highly available Mesos cluster.

There's more...

For more information regarding ZooKeeper configuration and administration, refer to http ://zookeeper.apache.org.

Configuring ZooKeeper on Ubuntu 14.04, 16.04, and OS X from source

Getting ready

Please follow the instructions in Chapter 1, *Getting Started with Apache Mesos* to install Mesos from source code prior to executing the following steps. For a multi-master Mesos/ZooKeeper configuration, confirm that DNS A (host) and PTR (reverse lookup) records have been added to your DNS servers for your Mesos hosts. DNS configuration is outside the scope of this book.

How to do it...

This recipe will work for both Ubuntu and OS X but we will use the following configuration on eight Ubuntu 16.04 VMs for our source install demo cluster:

Function	IP address	Hostname	Cluster	myid	Quorum
Master	10.10.0.92	ubuntu1692	MesosUbuntu16	92	2
Master	10.10.0.93	ubuntu1693	MesosUbuntu16	93	2
Master	10.10.0.94	ubuntu1694	MesosUbuntu16	94	2
Agent	10.10.0.95	ubuntu1695	N/A	N/A	N/A
Agent	10.10.0.96	ubuntu1696	N/A	N/A	N/A
Agent	10.10.0.97	ubuntu1697	N/A	N/A	N/A
Agent	10.10.0.98	ubuntu1698	N/A	N/A	N/A
Agent	10.10.0.99	ubuntu1699	N/A	N/A	N/A

Configuring Mesos masters with ZooKeeper

1. You will find the ZooKeeper directory in the 3rdparty subdirectory of the Mesos source directory. We recommend copying this directory to the location that you would like to run ZooKeeper, such as /usr/local or /opt, and then change into that directory. For example:

```
$ sudo cp -a ~/mesos-1.1.0/build/3rdparty/zookeeper-3.4.8
```

```
/usr/local/
$ sudo chown -R root.root /usr/local/zookeeper-3.4.8/
$ cd /usr/local/zookeeper-3.4.8/
```

2. Copy the `zoo_sample.cfg` file in the conf subdirectory of the `zookeeper` directory and create a `zoo.cfg` file in the same directory:

   ```
   $ sudo cp conf/zoo_sample.cfg conf/zoo.cfg
   ```

3. The source installation uses `/var/lib/zookeeper/` as the location for the `myid` file. Create the `/var/lib/zookeeper` directory and then create the `myid` file:

   ```
   $ sudo mkdir /var/lib/zookeeper
   $ sudo touch /var/lib/zookeeper/myid
   ```

4. Edit `/var/lib/zookeeper/myid` and add a unique integer between 1 and 255. If you plan on building a multi-master Mesos cluster, the integer in this file is arbitrary but it will need to be unique for each ZooKeeper instance on each Mesos master server. We will use the `myid` values in the previous chart for our example multi-master Mesos cluster.

5. Edit `~/zookeeper-3.4.8/conf/zoo.cfg` and change `dataDir=/tmp/zookeeper` to `dataDir=/var/lib/zookeeper`.

6. Edit `~/zookeeper-3.4.8/conf/zoo.cfg` and add a line for each ZooKeeper instance in your Mesos cluster. The integer that comes after `server` must match the integers in the `myid` files created in the previous steps for each ZooKeeper instance in your cluster. Here are examples for both single server and multi-master Mesos clusters:

   - **Example 1**:

     This is for a single Mesos/ZooKeeper instance on a development machine, so you would only need one line with the loopback address. The `myid` file (*step 4*) on this development machine would contain the integer `1`:

     ```
     server.1=127.0.0.1:2888:3888
     ```

- **Example 2**:

  This is for a Mesos production cluster with three Mesos/ZooKeeper masters. Each master node is running a ZooKeeper instance with a unique integer in the `myid` file. The numbers after the `server` entries must match the integers in the `myid` files for the three ZooKeeper servers. The three ZooKeeper servers in this example have `myid` file entries of `92`, `93`, and `94` respectively. Replace the IP address (`10.10.0.x`) in the examples below with the real IP addresses of your Mesos masters and use `myid` values of your choosing:

  ```
  server.92=10.10.0.92:2888:3888
  server.93=10.10.0.93:2888:3888
  server.94=10.10.0.94:2888:3888
  ```

 This author uses a `myid` strategy of using the last octet of the IP address as the `myid` for each server (as in the preceding example) to avoid confusion and simplify configuration. The `myid` is arbitrary and does not need to match the IP, but the `myid` integers for the masters **must** match the integers after `server` in the entries in `zoo.cfg`.

7. Configure all ZooKeeper/Mesos masters listed in the `zoo.cfg` file by following the previous steps prior to restarting Mesos with ZooKeeper on any of the servers. When all masters are configured, continue with the next step.

8. Stop any Mesos master and slave processes on each of the master servers if they are already running:

```
$ sudo killall mesos-master
$ sudo killall mesos-slave
```

9. Start ZooKeeper on each master server:

```
$ sudo ~/zookeeper-3.4.8/bin/zkServer.sh start
```

10. Now restart each Mesos master with ZooKeeper.

   To start our single Mesos master with ZooKeeper in development mode, we would execute:

```
$ ~/mesos-master --zk=zk://127.0.0.1:2181/mesos --ip=127.0.0.1 --
port=5050 --quorum=1 --log_dir=/var/log/mesos --
work_dir=/var/lib/mesos
```

To start our multi-master Mesos cluster with ZooKeeper, we would execute the following on each Mesos master, changing the `--ip=` and `--hostname=` values for each master server. This command will run the Mesos masters in the foreground so you will initially need to open several simultaneous terminal sessions to run all three masters:

```
$ ~/mesos-master --
zk=zk://10.10.0.92:2181,10.10.0.93:2181,10.10.0.94:2181/mesos --
port=5050 --quorum=2 --work_dir=/var/lib/mesos --ip=10.10.0.92 --
hostname=ubuntu1692 --cluster=MesosUbuntu16 --
log_dir=/var/log/mesos
```

After all Mesos masters are running, validate your cluster by pointing your browser to port `5050` on any of the master servers. Mesos masters running with ZooKeeper will only have one elected leader at a time. You can see which master is currently the leader by looking at the value for `Server:` in the upper-right corner of the Mesos UI:

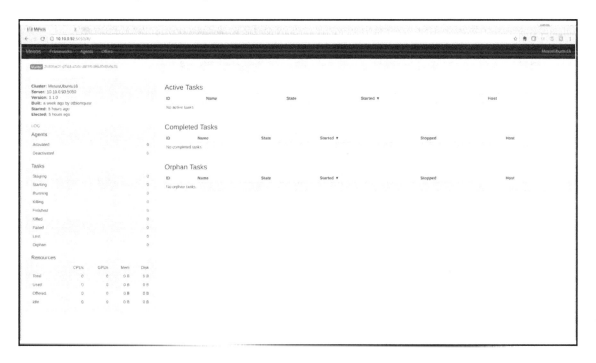

11. Once you are sure that your configuration is correct and the Mesos masters are running as expected, you can run the Mesos master processes in the background using the following commands:

    1. First, hit *Ctrl + C* to kill the foreground Mesos master processes. Then become the root user:

       ```
       $ sudo su -
       ```

    2. Execute this command to run the Mesos master in the background, changing the `--ip=` and `--hostname=` value for each master:

       ```
       $ nohup /opt/mesos-1.1.0/sbin/mesos-master --
       zk=zk://10.10.0.92:2181,10.10.0.93:2181,10.10.0.94:2181
       /mesos --port=5050 --quorum=2 --work_dir=/var/lib/mesos
       --ip=10.10.0.92 --hostname=ubuntu1692 --
       cluster=MesosUbuntu16 --log_dir=/var/log/mesos
       </dev/null >/dev/null 2>&1 &
       $ exit
       ```

Configuring Mesos agents with ZooKeeper

1. Stop any Mesos master and agent (slave) processes on the agent servers if they are already running:

   ```
   $ sudo killall mesos-master
   $ sudo killall mesos-slave
   ```

2. Start the Mesos agents on each agent server, changing the `--ip=` and `--hostname=` values for each server, and register them with the Zookeeper/Mesos masters. On our first Mesos agent server, we would execute:

   ```
   $ sudo ~/mesos-slave --
   master=zk://zk://10.10.0.92:2181,10.10.0.93:2181,10.10.0.94:218
   1/mesos --ip=10.10.0.95 --hostname=ubuntu1695 --
   log_dir=/var/log/mesos --work_dir=/var/lib/mesos
   ```

3. Validate that the agent is registered with the cluster by again pointing your browser to port 5050 on any one of the master servers. Then click on the **Agents** tab on the bar at the top of the Mesos UI. You should see the newly registered agent:

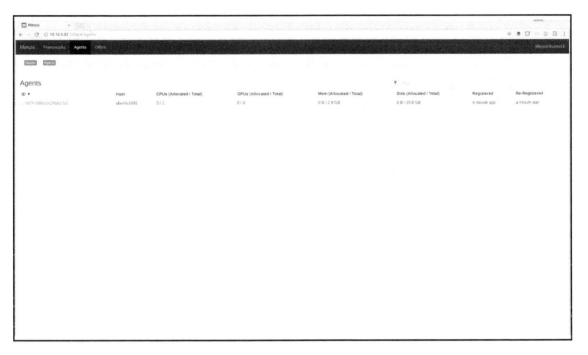

4. When you have confirmed that the agent is registered, you can run the Mesos agent processes in the background using the following commands.

   1. First, hit *Ctrl+C* to kill the foreground Mesos agent processes.

   2. Then become the root user:

   ```
   $ sudo su -
   ```

   3. Then execute this command to run the Mesos agent in the background, changing the `--ip=` and `--hostname=` value for each master:

   ```
   $ nohup ~/mesos-1.1.0/sbin/mesos-slave --
   master=zk://10.10.0.92:2181,10.10.0.93:2181,10.10.0.94:
   2181/mesos --work_dir=/var/lib/mesos --ip=10.10.0.95 --
   hostname=ubuntu1695 --log_dir=/var/log/mesos </dev/null
   >/dev/null 2>&1 &
   $ exit
   ```

5. Repeat *step 4* on all agent servers and validate:

How it works...

ZooKeeper is a Java application that is included with the Mesos source build so you do not need to compile it separately. Simply copy the files and run it from the directory of your choosing. Configuring Mesos with ZooKeeper will allow you to run a highly available Mesos cluster.

There's more...

For more information regarding ZooKeeper configuration and administration, refer to `http ://zookeeper.apache.org`.

3
Running and Maintaining Mesos

In this chapter, you will learn about the components of a Mesos cluster and how to configure them. The following are the recipes we will cover in this chapter:

- Logging and debugging
- Monitoring
- Setting attributes for agents
- Defining roles and resources
- Oversubscription
- Controlling permissions using access control lists
- Agent authentication
- Encryption SSL
- Upgrading Mesos

Introduction

Proper tool configuration is the key to running Mesos smoothly without any problems and with minimal operator assistance. A deep understanding of what each option means is required to provide the ideal configuration for a specific use case. There are over a hundred options to configure Mesos. Some of them accept Boolean values but most of them can have multiple values, which means there are countless ways to run Mesos. In Chapter 2, *Implementing High Availability with Apache ZooKeeper*, you have seen how to run Mesos in high availability mode. Here we will focus on more advanced options.

Logging and debugging

In this recipe, we will configure logging options that will allow us to debug the state of Mesos.

Getting ready

We will assume Mesos is available on localhost port 5050. The steps provided here will work for either master or agents.

How to do it...

When Mesos is installed from pre-built packages, the logs are by default stored in /var/log/mesos/. When installing from a source build, storing logs is disabled by default. To change the log store location, we need to edit /etc/default/mesos and set the LOGS variable to the desired destination. For some reason, mesos-init-wrapper does not transfer the contents of /etc/mesos/log_dir to the --log_dir flag. That's why we need to set the log's destination in the environment variable.

Remember that only Mesos logs will be stored there. Logs from third-party applications (for example, ZooKeeper) will still be sent to STDERR.

Changing the default logging level can be done in one of two ways: by specifying the --logging_level flag or by sending a request and changing the logging level at runtime for a specific period of time.

For example, to change the logging level to INFO, just put it in the following code:

```
/etc/mesos/logging_level
echo INFO > /etc/mesos/logging_level
```

The possible levels are INFO, WARNING, and ERROR.

For example, to change the logging level to the most verbose for 15 minutes for debug purposes, we need to send the following request to the logging/toggle endpoint:

```
curl -v -X POST localhost:5050/logging/toggle?level=3\&duration=15mins
```

How it works...

Mesos uses the `Google-glog` library for debugging, but third-party dependencies such as ZooKeeper have their own logging solution. All configuration options are backed by glog and apply only to Mesos core code.

Monitoring

In this recipe, we will set up monitoring for Mesos.

Getting ready

We must have a running monitoring ecosystem. Metrics storage could be a simple time-series database such as `graphite`, `influxdb`, or `prometheus`. In the following example, we are using graphite and our metrics are published with `http://diamond.readthedocs.io/en/latest/`.

How to do it...

Monitoring is enabled by default. Mesos does not provide any way to automatically push metrics to the registry. However, it exposes them as a JSON that can be periodically pulled and saved into the metrics registry:

1. Install Diamond using following command:

   ```
   pip install diamond
   ```

2. If additional packages are required to install them, run:

   ```
   sudo apt-get install python-pip python-dev build-essential.
   ```

   `pip` (Pip Installs Packages) is a Python package manager used to install software written in Python.

3. Configure the metrics handler and interval. Open
   `/etc/diamond/diamond.conf` and ensure that there is a section for graphite
   configuration:

   ```
   [handler_graphite]
   class = handlers.GraphiteHandler
   host = <graphite.host>
   port = <graphite.port>
   ```

   Remember to replace `graphite.host` and `graphite.port` with real
   graphite details.

4. Enable the default Mesos Collector. Create configuration files `diamond-setup -C MesosCollector`. Check whether the configuration has proper values and
   edit them if needed. The configuration can be found in
   `/etc/diamond/collectors/MesosCollector.conf`. On master, this file
   should look like this:

   ```
   enabled = True
   host = localhost
   port = 5050
   ```

   While on agent, the port could be different (`5051`), as follows:

   ```
   enabled = True
   host = localhost
   port = 5051
   ```

How it works...

Mesos exposes metrics via the HTTP API. Diamond is a small process that periodically pulls
metrics, parses them, and sends them to the metrics registry, in this case, graphite. The
default implementation of Mesos Collector does not store all the available metrics so it's
recommended to write a custom handler that will collect all the interesting information.

See also

Metrics could be read from the following endpoints:

- http://mesos.apache.org/documentation/latest/endpoints/metrics/snapshot/
- http://mesos.apache.org/documentation/latest/endpoints/slave/monitor/statistics/
- http://mesos.apache.org/documentation/latest/endpoints/slave/state/

Setting attributes for agents

In this recipe, we will set different attributes for our agents. Attributes are extremely useful when our cluster is not homogeneous and we want to distinguish agents from each other.

How to do it...

Let's assume our cluster contains agents with SSD and HDD drives. Disk resources will unify SSD and HDD, but from the user's perspective they are different and some tasks need to be run on SSD. We can label agents with the disk attributes hdd or ssd, depending on the disk type, hence allowing the user to decide which disk should be used for the job.

To create an attribute, we need to place the file in /etc/mesos-slave/attributes. The following command will create this directory:

```
mkdir -p /etc/mesos-slave/attributes
```

The filename will be the attribute label and the content will be a value. To create the disk:ssd attribute, simply create a file with the following contents:

```
echossd> /etc/mesos-slave/attributes/disk
```

How it works...

When Mesos presents offers to frameworks, each offer includes agent attributes so the framework can decide whether to accept or reject the offer.

Defining roles and resources

In this recipe, we will define roles and assign them weights to prioritize some frameworks over others.

How to do it...

Roles are part of the resources definition. We define resources and roles for each agent. For example, we want to change the default port range to `51000-52000` and the offered disk space to `4096` GB. To do this, we need to explicitly override the default values. You need to edit `/etc/mesos-slave/resources` and put the desired resources:

```
echo 'disk(*):4096; ports(*):[51000-52000]'> /etc/mesos-slave/resources
```

In a similar way, we can define other resources such as CPUs, memory, or GPUs just by adding the corresponding entry. The preceding configuration defines the default roles - `(*)`.

To assign the resource to a specific role, put the role name after the resource in brackets. For example, we want to run role development and test on one cluster. We want to distinguish ports offered to these roles. The development tasks will be run on ports `31000-32000` and be tested on `41000-42000`. To do it, we define the following resources:

```
echo 'ports(develop):[31000-32000]; ports(test):[41000-42000]'> /etc/mesos-slave/resources
```

With multiple frameworks deployed on Mesos, there is a chance that some of them are more important than others and should receive resource offers more often. We can achieve this with weighted roles.

Weights are configured with roles and mean what fraction of offers should be presented to frameworks with the given role. Offers will be presented proportionally more often to frameworks with higher weights. By default, each role has a weight of 1 but this could be changed using the Weights operator API.

To check configured weights, use `curl -X GET http://localhost:5050/weights`.

To change them, prepare the JSON file with weights definitions and send it with the HTTP
PUT method to the /weights endpoint. For example, to present the test role five times more
often than develop, we need to set a test role weight that is five times the weight of the role
test. So the weights.json file should look like this:

```
cat<< EOF >weights.json
    [
        {
"role": "develop",
"weight": 1.0
        },
        {
"role": "test",
"weight": 5.0
        }
    ]
EOF
```

Then we can send it to the master with:

```
curl -v -X PUT -d @weights.json http://localhost:5050/weights
```

How it works...

At startup, the Mesos agent performs checks and sets resources to default values that are
detected by the system. Those resources are then overridden with values provided by the
users. Resources are a part of the slave definition, so it might be necessary to clean the slave
metadata directory before starting it with a new configuration.

Roles are the way to customize how resources are offered to frameworks. Basically, roles
allow us to specify which resources should be used for specified purposes, so roles can be
used to divide clusters into dedicated parts, limit resource access, and provide quotas.

A role is just a label (string) that distinguishes framework resources. Each framework can
specify which role it wants to use. Currently, only one role per framework is supported
(https://issues.apache.org/jira/browse/MESOS-1763) and the framework needs to
specify it when it connects to the master. If the role is not named, * is used in place of the
role name; this means the resource is available for any role. If we specify the role name, only
that role can use the resource.

The weights API appeared in Mesos 1.0 and replaced the static weights definition with the command-line flag, which is now deprecated.

There's more...

Dynamic reservations

The way we defined roles earlier is called `static reservation`. This option is available only on agents and to change this setting, the agent must be drained and restarted. To prevent downtime, there is another way of creating reservations without downtime. It's similar to the weights definition because it uses the HTTP API. Reservations done with the HTTP API are called dynamic reservations because they can be done at runtime without any downtime. Frameworks can send requests to reserve and release unreserved resources. It's extremely useful with stateful applications and persistent storage, when the framework can dynamically reserve disk. With dynamic resources, comes the ability to label them. Those labels can be used by the framework to keep information about the purpose of the resource: `http://mesos.apache.org/documentation/latest/roles/`.

Persistent volumes

We can divide applications into two groups: stateless and stateful. With stateless applications, the application does some calculations based on one or more inputs and sends the results of this calculation to one or more outputs. So for the same data, it will do the same job any time it is run. Usually, these types of applications scale well and are easier to write and maintain. The second type of application is one that needs to store state. Databases are the best examples. A database is a special type of application where we store the state of our system. Databases store data on disk. In Mesos, when tasks complete or fail, all data created by these tasks could be deleted and therefore lost. There are two ways to handle that problem: we can use the shared filesystem or use the Mesos feature called persistent volumes.

The idea behind persistent volumes is quite easy. The framework can reserve some space for specific tasks and mark them as persistent volumes. This means when the task that is using this space terminates, the framework will get an offer containing a specific volume and will run this task again. Newly spawned tasks will get access to data created by the previously terminated task, so they can restore state.

Persistent volumes are based on a reservation system, which is designed to reserve certain resources for frameworks with specific roles. Reservations can be either dynamic or static. Dynamic reservation means the reservations are created dynamically by the framework. This does not require any other integration in `mesos` options, other than setting proper ACLs for the framework role. Static reservation means reservations are planned before `mesos` is started. Role reservation is provided in `--resources`, so the first step to enable persistent volumes is to configure the roles of your framework, and the framework should automatically create volumes if needed.

Oversubscription

In this recipe, you will learn how to turn on oversubscription, a module that enables Mesos to make use of allocated but unused resources.

How to do it...

Mesos comes with the basic implementation of the resource estimator and QoS controller, provided the estimator returns a fixed value each time. The QoS controller is a little bit more advanced because it monitors the system and revokes all slack resources when the system load is too high:

```
system load is too high:
echoorg_apache_mesos_FixedResourceEstimator> /etc/mesos-
slave/resource_estimator
echoorg_apache_mesos_LoadQoSController> /etc/mesos-slave/qos_controller
echo 60secs > /etc/mesos-slave/qos_correction_interval_min
cat<< EOF > /etc/mesos-slave/modules
{
"libraries":[
        {
"file":"/usr/lib/mesos/modules/libload_qos_controller.so",
"modules":{
"name":"org_apache_mesos_LoadQoSController",
"parameters":[
            {
"key":"load_threshold_5min",
"value":"6"
                },
                {
"key":"load_threshold_15min",
"value":"4"
                }
```

```
                    ]
                }
            },
            {
    "file":"/usr/lib/mesos/modules/libfixed_resource_estimator.so",
    "modules":{
    "name":"org_apache_mesos_FixedResourceEstimator",
    "parameters":{
    "key":"resources",
    "value":"cpus:4"
                    }
                }
            }
        ]
    }
    EOF
```

Then in the `master` log, we should see that the agent is offering revocable resources labeled with REV:

```
I0717 21:47:30.850740 17026 master.cpp:5128] Received update of agent
f196f4e6-1631-445f-8403-9b5e564a8111-S2 at slave(1)@127.0.1.1:5051
(10.10.10.10) with total oversubscribed resources cpus(*){REV}:4
```

How it works...

Oversubscription is a mechanism to allocate more resources than are available on the cluster. It takes advantage of the fact that allocated resources are usually not fully utilized. This means we could create tasks utilizing these slack resources. The main advantage of this approach is we can have higher total hardware utilization, but it comes with a price. When the task needs all its allocated resources, the slack task must be deleted to give the resources back. Currently, only Aurora (see https://issues.apache.org/jira/browse/AURORA-1343) supports this feature. A framework can schedule slack tasks only if it communicates with Mesos through the HTTP API. There is a difference between used, allocated, and available resources. Wasted resources could be used by enabling oversubscription:

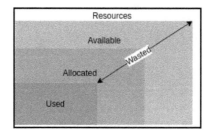

The QoS controller is responsible for monitoring slack tasks and removes them if they decrease the performance of other tasks. The resource estimator monitors the available resources and decides how many slack resources can be presented to frameworks.

See also

- https://mesosphere.com/blog/2015/08/26/turbocharging-your-mesos-cluster-with-oversubscription/
- https://www.youtube.com/watch?v=yVSWQG7N_F8
- https://www.youtube.com/watch?v=dvrJp85PDLQ
- https://github.com/mesosphere/serenity

Controlling permissions using access control lists

In this recipe, you will learn how to control the permissions of principals (users and frameworks).

Getting ready

You need to identify the principals of your cluster. This consists of groups and users who operate Mesos and frameworks that interact with it. In the following example, we will assume that we operate a single framework that can only use the services role.

How to do it...

Mesos reads **Access Control List's (ACL)** configuration from a JSON file. Each action is a key that contains an array of JSON objects, pairing principals with the object on which actions are performed:

```
cat << EOF > /etc/mesos-master/acls
{
"register_frameworks":[    # configure principals who can register
frameworks
    {
principals":{       # set principals who can
```

```
    "values":[
    "marathon"      # register frameworks to 'marathon'
            ]
        },
    "roles":{          # limit roles that could be used
    "values":[        # to register to 'services'
    "services"
            ]
        }
    },
    {
    "principals":{
    "type":"NONE"     # refuse other principals to register
        },
    "roles":{          # frameworks with 'services' role
    "values":[
    "services"
            ]
        }
    }
    ]
}
EOF
```

How it works...

ACLs could be used as an authorization engine. They allows you to explicitly exclude specific principals from performing actions. ACLs provide fine-grained access control. JSON describes the desired action. Each action can be controlled and limited to None, Any, or specified frameworks.

The preceding configuration declares that the principal marathon can register frameworks with role services, but no other principal can do it.

The file structure is simple. It's mapped from authorizable action to a list of rules. Each rule contains the affected principals and object that is protected; typically a resource or user.

To mention a specific principal, we need to provide its name in the principals.values lists, or we can use one of the two quantifiers:

- "type":"NONE": This matches no principals/roles
- "type":"ANY": This matches all principals/roles

The order of the rules and entries is important as succeeding entries in the preceding example do not overwrite the entries defined earlier. If we swap entries in the preceding example, we will prevent all principals from registering the framework with the services role.

Currently, there are authorizable actions and all of them are described in the document available at http://mesos.apache.org/documentation/latest/authorization/.

Agent authentication

In this recipe, you will learn how to authenticate agents to prevent alien agents and frameworks joining the cluster.

Getting ready

Before we start configuring authentication, we need to identify the principals of our cluster and generate secrets for them. In the following example, we assume we have two principal marathon (framework) and agent (all agents).

How to do it...

To enable authentication, we need to define which authentication mechanism we want to use. In this example, we will use CRAM-MD5, which is built into Mesos and is, in fact, quite a popular authentication algorithm used in SMTP and LDAP.

Master

Enable authentication of frameworks and agents by setting:

```
echo true > /etc/mesos-master/authenticate_frameworks
echo true > /etc/mesos-master/authenticate_agents
```

Choose CRAM-MD5 as an authenticator:

```
echo crammd5 > /etc/mesos-master/authenticators
```

Create a file with the principals' secrets. Secrets provided by the principal will be checked against this file during authentication:

```
mkdir -p /etc/mesos-master/confcat << EOF > /etc/mesos-
master/conf/credentials.json
{
"credentials" : [
      {
"principal": "marathon",
"secret": "marathon_secret"
      },
      {
"principal": "agent",
"secret": "agents_secret"
     }
   ]
 }
EOF
```

The credentials file should have the minimal possible access rights since it contains secrets:

```
chmod 600 /etc/mesos-master/conf/credentials.json
```

Tell the master where the credentials file is located:

```
echo /etc/mesos-master/conf/credentials.json>
/etc/mesos-master/credentials
```

Agent

Create a file with the agent's secrets. This file will be used to authenticate to the master:

```
mkdir -p /etc/mesos-slave/confcat << EOF > /etc/mesos-
slave/conf/credential.json
{
"principal": "agent",
 "secret": "agents_secret"
  }
EOF
chmod 600 /etc/mesos-slave/conf/credential.json
```

Tell the agent where the credentials file is located:

```
echo /etc/mesos-slave/conf/credential.json>
/etc/mesos-slave/credential
```

Marathon

Marathon accepts credentials in a different manner to Mesos. Instead of storing everything in one file, only secrets are stored in the file. The principal is passed by the command-line flag.

1. Put the marathon secret in the file:

   ```
   echo marathon_secret>/etc/marathon/mesos_authentication_secret
   ```

2. Tell marathon where the credentials file is located:

   ```
   echo /etc/marathon/mesos_authentication_secret>
   /etc/marathon/conf/mesos_authentication_secret_file
   ```

3. Set the principal:

   ```
   echo marathon > /etc/marathon/conf/mesos_authentication_principal
   ```

How it works...

To prevent the launch of unauthorized frameworks, we can specify a secret that needs to be passed by the framework to be accepted by Mesos. The Scheduler API accepts the principal and secret as a way of authenticating frameworks. The same approach applies to agents. Only those that know the secret can join the cluster.

It's recommended to set the minimum possible file permissions on files containing secrets. Secrets are provided by the file to prevent them appearing in logs.

Encryption SSL

In this recipe, you will learn how to make communication secure and limit the possibility of eavesdropping by enabling SSL.

Getting ready

Prepare certificates for encryption. We assume they are stored in `/etc/mesos/conf/ssl/key` and `/etc/mesos/conf/ssl/cert.pem`.

If you don't have certificates, you can create some with the following commands. Remember certificates are prepared only for example purposes and should not be used in a production environment:

```
mkdir -p /etc/mesos/conf/ssl
opensslreq -batch -nodes -new -x509 -keyout
/etc/mesos/conf/ssl/key.pem
-out /etc/mesos/conf/ssl/cert.pem
```

If you want to build Mesos from source with SSL enabled, configure the source code with the following options before you build it:

```
./configure --enable-libevent --enable-ssl.
```

How to do it...

To enable SSL, add the following lines to /etc/default/mesos:

```
SSL_ENABLED=1
SSL_KEY_FILE=/etc/mesos/conf/ssl/key.pem
SSL_CERT_FILE=/etc/mesos/conf/ssl/cert.pem
SSL_REQUIRE_CERT=false
```

How it works...

In the preceding configuration example, we tell Mesos to use the provided certificates to validate itself to the client and encrypt transmission. It's important to use trusted certificates so that clients can validate them. In this example configuration, Mesos does not require client-side certificates to authenticate the client. To require client-side certificates, we need to set SSL_REQUIRE_CERT=true. Remember that this setting will occur for all endpoints and all clients, so the web UI may not work in most browsers, because we're using a self-signed certificate in this example.

Remember that your frameworks and tools need to support SSL. To enable support for both SSL and plain communication, set SSL_SUPPORT_DOWNGRADE=true.

Upgrading Mesos

In this recipe, you will learn how to upgrade your Mesos cluster.

How to do it...

Mesos release cadence is at least one release per quarter. Minor releases are backward compatible, although there could be some small incompatibilities or the dropping of deprecated methods. The recommended method of upgrading is to apply all intermediate versions. For example, to upgrade from `0.27.2` to `1.0.0`, we should apply `0.28.0`, `0.28.1`, `0.28.2`, and finally `1.0.0`.

If the agent's configuration changes, clearing the `metadata` directory is required. You can do this with the following code:

```
rm -rv {MESOS_DIR}/metadata
```

Here, `{MESOS_DIR}` should be replaced with the configured Mesos directory.

Rolling upgrades is the preferred method of upgrading clusters, starting with masters and then agents.

To minimize the impact on running tasks, if an agent's configuration changes and it becomes inaccessible, then it should be switched to maintenance mode.

How it works...

Configuration changes may require clearing the metadata because the changes may not be backward compatible. For example, when an agent runs with different isolators, it shouldn't attach to the already running processes without this isolator. The Mesos architecture will guarantee that the executors that were not attached to the Mesos agent will commit suicide after a configurable amount of time (`--executor_registration_timeout`).

Maintenance mode allows you to declare the time window during which the agent will be inaccessible. When this occurs, Mesos will send a reverse offer to all the frameworks to drain that particular agent. Each frameworks are responsible for shutting down its task and spawning it on another agent. The Maintenance mode is applied, even if the framework does not implement the HTTP API or is explicitly declined. Using maintenance mode can prevent restarting tasks multiple times.

Consider the following example with five agents and one task, X. We schedule the rolling upgrade of all the agents. Task X is deployed on agent 1. When it goes down, it's moved to 2, then to 3, and so on. This approach is extremely inefficient because the task is restarted five times, but it only needs to be restarted twice. Maintenance mode enables the framework to optimally schedule the task to run on agent 5 when 1 goes down, and then return to 1 when 5 goes down:

Worst case scenario of rolling upgrade without maintenance mode legend optimal solution of rolling upgrade with maintenance mode.

4
Understanding the Scheduler API

In this chapter, you will learn about the frameworks and how they interact with Mesos. To do this, we will develop a simple framework.

The following are the recipes covered in this chapter:

- Installing Protobuf
- Registering frameworks
- Handling events
- Declining offers
- Scheduling tasks
- Acknowledging task updates
- Killing tasks
- State persistence
- Reconciliation

Introduction

The following recipes will guide you through creating a simple **Mesos** framework. It's important that this framework is prepared to be as simple as possible, just to demonstrate how frameworks interact with Mesos. However, the price of simplicity is robustness. It's not designed to handle production traffic but could be used as a starting point for creating real-world solutions.

Our framework will be created in Go. Go is getting more and more popular in system infrastructure, mostly because it gives C/C++ system performance with syntax and memory management known from higher-level languages such as Python. Another point in its favor is a powerful standard library. Our framework will require only one external dependency, Protobuf: `https://github.com/golang/protobuf`.

In our implementation, we will use the Mesos HTTP API. It's worth mentioning that this API is by design not RESTful, but still pretty easy to use.

Before you start, install Go on your machine and create a new directory where we can keep all the framework files.

Installing Protobuf

In this recipe, we will be installing **Protobuf** to generate **Golang** structures used in communication with Mesos.

Getting ready

Install Golang, Protobuf, and the Golang Protobuf bindings:

```
sudo add-apt-repository ppa:ubuntu-lxc/lxd-stable
sudo apt-get update
sudo apt-get install golang git
export GOPATH=~/go
export PATH=$PATH:$GOPATH/bin
sudo apt-get install protobuf-compiler
go get -u github.com/golang/protobuf/{proto,protoc-gen-go}
```

How to do it...

1. Create a project directory and go there:

```
mkdir -p $GOPATH/src/simple-scheduler
cd $GOPATH/src/simple-scheduler
```

2. Download the Mesos protobuf message definitions:

```
wget
https://raw.githubusercontent.com/apache/mesos/170ac/include/mesos/
v1/mesos.proto
wget
https://raw.githubusercontent.com/apache/mesos/170ac/include/mesos/
v1/scheduler/scheduler.proto
```

3. Tweak them to our needs. Change the default package of generated bindings to one that matches Golang. We will keep the whole project in one main package and the generated bindings should fit in it. To make this, apply the following patches to `scheduler.proto` and `mesos.proto`:

```
cat <<EOF | patch
--- mesos.proto 2016-07-28 00:39:01.644273001 +0200
+++ mesos.proto 2016-08-08 22:16:37.112678075 +0200
@@ -18,6 +18,7 @@

option java_package = "org.apache.mesos.v1";
option java_outer_classname = "Protos";
+option go_package = "main";


/**
EOF

cat <<EOF | patch
--- scheduler.proto 2016-08-08 22:16:30.372706543 +0200
+++ scheduler.proto 2016-07-28 00:39:39.244296938 +0200
@@ -14,12 +14,13 @@
// See the License for the specific language governing permissions
and
// limitations under the License.

-import "mesos/v1/mesos.proto";
+import "mesos.proto";

-package mesos.v1.scheduler;
+package mesos.v1;

option java_package = "org.apache.mesos.v1.scheduler";
option java_outer_classname = "Protos";
+option go_package = "main";

/**
EOF
```

4. Generate bindings for Mesos Protobuf messages:

```
protoc --go_out=. *.proto
```

5. As a result, the working directory should have the following content:

```
mesos.pb.go mesos.proto scheduler.pb.go scheduler.proto
```

6. And when we try to build the project with `go build`, we should get the following error:

```
# github.com/janisz/mesos-cookbook/4_understanding_frameworks
runtime.main: call to external function main.main
runtime.main: main.main: not defined
runtime.main: undefined: main.main
```

This is an expected error since we have only declared the data transfer object.

How it works...

Protobufs are a technology to serialize structured data. It was developed at Google to provide an easy-to-use, language-agnostic way to describe data that is consumed and produced by the system. Besides the serialization standard, it allows for validation of the structure of messages and backward compatibility of schema. It could be compared to XML, but it was designed to be smaller and easier to write and understand. Protocol buffers comes with a binary serializer as well as JSON.

Mesos uses Protobuf to specify schema for all data transfer objects. In this recipe, we compile that schema from proto files to Go language structures. Now we can use these structures to easily interact with Mesos.

Registering frameworks

In this recipe, we will learn how frameworks register in Mesos to receive offers and state updates.

How to do it...

We will create the `scheduler.go` file and implement our framework inside of it.

Before we start, we need to define some globals and imports that we will need later:

```
import (
        "bufio"
        "bytes"
        "log"
        "net/http"
        "os"
        "strconv"
        "strings"
        "github.com/golang/protobuf/jsonpb"
)
// Url to Mesos master scheduler API
const schedulerApiUrl = "http://10.10.10.10:5050/api/v1/scheduler"
// Current framework configuration
var frameworkInfo FrameworkInfo
// Marshaler to serialize Protobuf Message to JSON
var marshaller = jsonpb.Marshaler{
        EnumsAsInts: false,
        Indent: " ",
        OrigName: true,
}
```

`jsonpb.Marshaler` is a part of the Golang Protobuf binding. It's responsible for converting structs into JSON. We will use it to serialize the messages we send to Mesos. It's important to use a proper `Marshaler` because, as you can see, generated structs have additional `struct` tags with serialization hints. For example, enums are stored as integers but Mesos requires them as text; the default JSON `Marshaler` will ignore these hints and pass them as `Ints`.

The next step is to define the `main()` function. In `main`, we will populate `frameworkInfo` with the values required to register the framework. In this simple example, we don't use security features or roles, but if we do, `frameworkInfo` is the place where this could be set:

```
func main() {
    user := "root"
    name := "simple_framework"
    hostname, err := os.Hostname()
    if err != nil {
            log.Fatal(err)
    }
    frameworkInfo = FrameworkInfo{
        User: &user,
        Name: &name,
        Hostname: &hostname,
        FailoverTimeout: &failoverTimeout,
        Checkpoint: &checkpoint,
```

```
        }
            log.Fatal(subscribe())
    }
```

In the last line, we call the `subscribe()` function. Now it's time to implement it. This will be the biggest function. In the book example, we skipped error handling but remember that it's an important part of writing robust software in Go:

```
func subscribe() error {
        subscribeCall := &Call{
                Type: Call_SUBSCRIBE.Enum(),
                Subscribe: &Call_Subscribe{FrameworkInfo: &frameworkInfo},
        }
        body, _ := marshaller.MarshalToString(subscribeCall)
        log.Print(body)
        res, _ := http.Post(schedulerApiUrl, "application/json",
bytes.NewBuffer([]byte(body)))
        defer res.Body.Close()

        reader := bufio.NewReader(res.Body)
        // Read line from Mesos
        line, _ := reader.ReadString('\n')
        // First line contains numbers of message bytes
        bytesCount, _ := strconv.Atoi(strings.Trim(line, "\n"))
        // Event loop
        for {
            // Read line from Mesos
            line, _ = reader.ReadString('\n')
            line = strings.Trim(line, "\n")
            // Read important data
            data := line[:bytesCount]
            // Rest data will be bytes of next message
            bytesCount, _ = strconv.Atoi((line[bytesCount:]))
            // Do not handle events, just log them
            log.Printf("Got: [%s]", data)
        }
    }
```

We run our framework with:

```
go run scheduler.go scheduler.pb.go mesos.pb.go
```

It should appear on the **Frameworks** tab in the Mesos UI. After a while, we will see that it has allocated some resources and also see pending offers in the Offers tab in the Mesos UI:

How it works...

Framework registration in Mesos terminology is equivalent to subscribing to events. There are eight types of event and so far we are not handling any of them. That's why we can see a pending offer on our framework.

Handling events

In this recipe, we will learn how Mesos notifies frameworks about updates.

How to do it...

To handle events, we need to parse data that we obtain from Mesos. To do that, add the following code at the end of the loop in the `subscribe()` function:

```
var event Event
sonpb.UnmarshalString(data, &event)
log.Printf("Got: [%s]", event.String())
```

After parsing, we need to handle events that can vary in type. To do this, we will use the `switch` control statement on the event type:

```
switch *event.Type {
case Event_SUBSCRIBED:
        log.Print("Subscribed")
        frameworkInfo.Id = event.Subscribed.FrameworkId
        mesosStreamID = res.Header.Get("Mesos-Stream-Id")
case Event_HEARTBEAT:
        log.Print("PING")
}
```

Remember to declare the global `mesosStreamID` variable:

```
var mesosStreamID string
```

How it works...

Events come with persistent HTTP connection one-by-one. Protobuf binding comes with the method to parse the data into Golang structs. Then in our event loop, we can perform specific actions depending on event type.

In this example, we are not doing any sophisticated actions. We just log the event that occurs and keep `FrameworkID` and `mesosStreamID` assigned to variables. These two identifiers are important for communication with Mesos. Every future request to Mesos must contain `FrameworkID`, which is quite obvious because Mesos must know who it is talking to, and `mesosStreamID` is used by Mesos to distinguish different framework instances.

In our example, we will run only one instance of the framework, but it's good practice to run more of them to allow a framework to be available when one instance goes down.

In this example, we are handling `HEARTBEAT`. This is the event that is used to inform frameworks that the connection is still alive. Again, we only log that this event occurs, but in the real world we should store information about how often the event will be sent by the framework and if we don't receive it in the specified time, we should perform re-registration.

Declining offers

In this recipe, we will handle offers by declining them so they can be presented to other frameworks.

How to do it...

So far, our framework has been acquiring resources, although it's not using them. This is because it gets offers but does not respond to them. To make offers free, we need to explicitly refuse them.

To refuse `Offers`, we need to handle the `Offers` event. We can do this by adding the following code in the `event` type switch:

```
case Event_OFFERS:
        log.Printf("Handle offers returns: %v",
handleOffers(event.Offers))
```

Of course, we need to implement the `handleOffers()` function. But before that, we should prepare the `call()` function, which will be useful for implementation. This function will be used to send messages to Mesos:

```
func call(message *Call) error {
        message.FrameworkId = frameworkInfo.Id
        body, _ := marshaller.MarshalToString(message)
        req, _ := http.NewRequest("POST", schedulerApiUrl,
bytes.NewBuffer([]byte(body)))
        req.Header.Set("Mesos-Stream-Id", mesosStreamID)
        req.Header.Set("Content-Type", "application/json")
        log.Printf("Call %s %s", message.Type, string(body))
        res, _ := http.DefaultClient.Do(req)
        defer res.Body.Close()
        if res.StatusCode != 202 {
```

```
                io.Copy(os.Stderr, res.Body)
                return fmt.Errorf("Error %d", res.StatusCode)
        }
        return nil
}
```

The structure of the preceding function is simple. Take the message from the argument and enhance it with `FrameworkID` and `mesosStreamID` that we obtained from the `subscribe` event.

Finally, we can implement `handleOffers()`, which for now will decline all offers it received:

```
func handleOffers(offers *Event_Offers) error {
        offerIds := []*OfferID{}
        for _, offer := range offers.Offers {
        offerIds = append(offerIds, offer.Id)
        }
        decline := &Call{
                Type: Call_DECLINE.Enum(),
                Decline: &Call_Decline{OfferIds: offerIds},
        }
        return call(decline)
}
```

Remember, to import packages we just use – `fmt` and `io`.

How it works...

After getting resource offers from Mesos, we extract their IDs and send decline messages for all offers. After that operation, Mesos marks the resources as free and can present them to other frameworks.

In the Mesos UI, we can see that our framework periodically has some resources attached to it, but after a while it reports that it uses nothing. On the **Offers** tab, we can see that offers appear but after a while they disappear. This means we correctly declined them:

Scheduling tasks

In this recipe, we will ask Mesos to run a task.

How to do it...

First of all, we need to know what task we want to schedule. To allow communication with the framework, we will prepare the HTTP API.

To handle HTTP requests, we need to implement the HTTP handler and bind it to some ports.

Let's declare the following variables in the main() function:

```
listen := ":9090"
webuiURL := fmt.Sprintf("http://%s%s", hostname, listen)
```

Let's also declare one global variable:

```
var taskID uint64
```

Tasks can be launched only when offers are available. To communicate with the offer handler, we will use a channel. If you are not familiar with Golang channels, they're similar to a message queue or pipe. Basically, you write at one end and read at another. Let's declare it globally:

```
var commandChan = make(chan string, 100)
```

Extend the FrameworkInfo definition with the just-created web UI URL:

```
frameworkInfo = FrameworkInfo{
        User: &user,
        Name: &name,
        Hostname: &hostname,
        WebuiUrl: &webuiURL,
}
```

Next, we need to start the HTTP handler before we call subscribe():

```
http.HandleFunc("/", web)
go func() {
        log.Fatal(http.ListenAndServe(listen, nil))
}()
```

Then, implement the `web` function:

```
func web(w http.ResponseWriter, r *http.Request) {
    r.ParseForm()
    switch r.Method {
    case "POST":
        cmd := r.Form["cmd"][0]
        commandChan <- cmd
        w.WriteHeader(http.StatusAccepted)
        fmt.Fprintf(w, "Scheduled: %s", cmd)
    default:
        http.Error(w, "Method Not Allowed", http.StatusMethodNotAllowed)
    }
}
```

To keep the project small, we will assume that each task requires the same resources. To keep it even simpler, we won't require ports. Let's define the function that will return default resources for the task:

```
func defaultResources() []*Resource {
    CPU := "cpus"
    MEM := "mem"
    cpu := float64(0.1)

    return []*Resource{
        {
            Name: &CPU,
            Type: Value_SCALAR.Enum(),
            Scalar: &Value_Scalar{Value: &cpu},
        },
        {
            Name: &MEM,
            Type: Value_SCALAR.Enum(),
            Scalar: &Value_Scalar{Value: &cpu},
        },
    }
}
```

We have all the pieces ready to launch our tasks. We will do this in the previously defined `handleOffers` function:

```
func handleOffers(offers *Event_Offers) error {

    offerIds := []*OfferID{}
    for _, offer := range offers.Offers {
        offerIds = append(offerIds, offer.Id)
    }
```

```
                  select {
                  case cmd := <-commandChan:
                          firstOffer := offers.Offers[0]

                          TRUE := true
                          newTaskID := fmt.Sprint(atomic.AddUint64(&taskID, 1))
                          taskInfo := []*TaskInfo{{
                                  Name: &cmd,
                                  TaskId: &TaskID{
                                          Value: &newTaskID,
                                  },
                                  AgentId: firstOffer.AgentId,
                                  Resources: defaultResources(),
                                  Command: &CommandInfo{
                                          Shell: &TRUE,
                                          Value: &cmd,
                          }}}
                      accept := &Call{
                              Type: Call_ACCEPT.Enum(),
                              Accept: &Call_Accept{
                                  OfferIds: offerIds,
                                  Operations: []*Offer_Operation{{
                                          Type: Offer_Operation_LAUNCH.Enum(),
                                          Launch: &Offer_Operation_Launch{
                                                  TaskInfos: taskInfo,
                                          }}}}}
                          return call(accept)
                  default:
                        decline := &Call{
                                Type: Call_DECLINE.Enum(),
                                Decline: &Call_Decline{OfferIds: offerIds},
                        }
                          return call(decline)
                  }
          }
```

Remember to import the package we just used: `sync/atomic`.

How it works...

Launching tasks combines two functionalities of the framework: interaction with Mesos and with the user. For example, the user sends a launch task request to start the HTTP server on port 9033:

```
curl -X POST
"http://localhost:9090/?cmd=python%20-m%20SimpleHTTPServer%209033"
```

Here, the request is parsed and the command is passed to handle the offers function via the channel.

Offers handling doesn't change much. If there is no request from the user, the offer is declined. When any command appears on the channel, it's packed in an `accept` request with default resources and sent to Mesos.

Each task must have its own ID generated by the framework. In our example, we are incrementing the `taskID` variable so tasks will be given numbers starting from 1.

Acknowledging task updates

In this recipe, we will learn how Mesos communicates the task's state changes and how to handle these changes.

How to do it...

Right now, we should be able to spawn new tasks on a Mesos cluster but when we deploy tasks with an invalid command, such as `false`:

```
curl -X POST "http://localhost:9090/?cmd=false"
```

This task immediately ends with an exit code equal to 1. In the Mesos UI, we can see these tasks have failed but it's not presented in completed tasks. This is because each task state update needs to be acknowledged by the framework.

In the `subscribe` event switch, add the following case:

```
case Event_UPDATE:
    log.Printf("Handle update returns: %v", handleUpdate(event.Update))
```

Then implement the `handleUpdate` function:

```
func handleUpdate(update *Event_Update) error {
    return call(&Call{
        Type: Call_ACKNOWLEDGE.Enum(),
        Acknowledge: &Call_Acknowledge{
            AgentId: update.Status.AgentId,
            TaskId: update.Status.TaskId,
            Uuid: update.Status.Uuid,
        },
    })
}
```

How it works...

Mesos HTTP calls are processed asynchronously, apart from `subscribe`, which is used to `push` events to the framework. Task state changes are similar to offers. Offers must be explicitly declined or accepted. The same thing happens with task updates. Each update must be acknowledged by the framework so Mesos can mark it with this state. The only status that does not need to be acknowledged is `TASK LOST`. Our framework will send an acknowledgment for `TASK LOST` too, but since the update event for `TASK LOST` does not contain a `UUID`, it will be declined by Mesos, which we can observe in the logs.

Killing tasks

In this recipe, we will ask Mesos to shut down a task.

How to do it...

Killing tasks is similar to launching tasks with one difference: tasks can be killed at any time.

Let's add support for the `delete` method in the `web` function:

```
case "DELETE":
    id := r.Form["id"][0]
    err := kill(id)
    if err != nil {
            fmt.Fprint(w, err)
    } else {
            fmt.Print(w, "KILLED")
    }
```

We need to implement the `kill` function. It'll be similar to acknowledge because it will only prepare and send a message to Mesos. To kill tasks, we need to know the task's ID. We will get it from the user and agent ID on which the task is launched. We need to modify our framework to keep track of the launched tasks. We will keep that in the global map, where task ID will be the `key` and `task` last update will be the value:

```
var tasksState = make(map[string]*TaskStatus)
```

This map will be updated every time we get an update. So in the `hadleUpdate()` function, we need to add the following:

```
tasksState[update.Status.TaskId.GetValue()] = update.Status
```

Now we have all the required data to perform the kill:

```
func kill(id string) error {
    update, ok := tasksState[id]
    log.Printf("Kill task %s [%#v]", id, update)
  if !ok {
    return fmt.Errorf("Unknown task %s", id)
  }
   return call(&Call{
      Type: Call_KILL.Enum(),
      Kill: &Call_Kill{
          TaskId: update.TaskId,
          AgentId: update.AgentId,
      },
   })
}
```

To make the framework more useful, we can implement the `HTTP GET` method, which will return the framework state:

```
case "GET":
    stateJSON, _ := json.Marshal(tasksState)
    w.Header().Add("Content-type", "application/json")
    fmt.Fprint(w, string(stateJSON))
```

Remember to import the package we just used: `encoding/json`.

How it works...

Refer to the following steps:

1. Schedule a new task:

   ```
   curl -X POST
   "http://localhost:9090/?cmd=python%20-m%20SimpleHTTPServer%209033"
   ```

2. Wait until it starts and appears in response to `GET`:

   ```
   curl -X GET "http://localhost:9090"
   ```

3. Then, kill it:

```
curl -X DELETE "http://localhost:9090/?id=1"
```

Then you should see your tasks in the completed tasks section with the status KILLED.

Killing tasks is probably as important as launching them. To kill a task, we need to provide the task ID and agent ID. Task kill is immutable. No matter how many times we call it, the final state will always be the same: TASK KILLED. After killing a task, a task executor sends an update to the Mesos agent, which passes it to the Mesos master, which eventually pushes the task update event to the framework. This looks over-engineered but makes Mesos fault tolerant and reduces executor code, because the Mesos slave takes care of all communication with the Mesos master, including error handling.

State persistence

In this recipe, we will learn how to persist framework state between restarts.

How to do it...

Every time we restart our framework, it starts from scratch, losing all information about the tasks it's scheduled. After the framework goes down, Mesos kills all its tasks. This behavior is not acceptable when we want to upgrade the framework without restarting its tasks. To change this, we must do two things: tell Mesos to keep tasks after framework communication fails, and keep framework state between restarts.

In the main() function, declare the variable holding the framework failover seconds and checkpointing flag:

```
failoverTimeout := float64(3600)
checkpoint := true
```

We will use them in the framework info declaration.

Then we need to store the framework info and task state. The framework info is changed only after the subscribe method. After subscription, it's worthwhile saving, since it contains a framework that is required to reconnect.

Declare a global variable with a path to framework info files:

```
var frameworkInfoFile = fmt.Sprintf("%s/%s", os.TempDir(),
"framewrok.json")
```

In the `main` function, read this file:

```
frameworkJSON, err := ioutil.ReadFile(frameworkInfoFile)
if err == nil {
        jsonpb.UnmarshalString(string(frameworkJSON), &frameworkInfo)
} else {
        frameworkInfo = FrameworkInfo{
                User:            &user,
                Name:            &name,
                Hostname:    &hostname,
                WebuiUrl:    &webuiURL,
                FailoverTimeout: &failoverTimeout,
            Checkpoint: &checkpoint,
        }
}
```

Save `frameworkInfo` to the file in the `subscribe` function just after the `frameworkId` is stored in framework info:

```
json, _ := marshaller.MarshalToString(&frameworkInfo)
ioutil.WriteFile(frameworkInfoFile, []byte(json), 0644)
```

We must extend the `subscribe` message with the `frameworkId` in order to create a valid message:

```
subscribeCall := &Call{
FrameworkId: frameworkInfo.Id,
Type: Call_SUBSCRIBE.Enum(),
Subscribe: &Call_Subscribe{FrameworkInfo: &frameworkInfo},
}
```

How it works...

The framework failover time defines how long Mesos should keep tasks of specific frameworks alive after these time tasks and executors are killed. By default, it's set to 0 and that's why, when we restarted the framework, all the tasks were gone.

`Checkpoint` is a flag that asks agents to save the executor's state on disk. This allows agents to attach to executors after a restart and recovery state.

When the framework registers, providing a `frameworkId`, Mesos knows it's a new instance of the old framework and does not assign a new ID for it, although a new `mesosStreamID` will be generated since it will be discovered as a new instance.

Reconciliation

In this recipe, we will learn how to reconcile the state between the framework and Mesos.

How to do it...

Although our tasks persist after the framework restarts, they cannot be managed because the framework does not know about them. To make it aware of tasks it had scheduled previously, we need to keep them between restarts. We will do it in the same way as framework info. We will store the task state after every update and load it after registration.

Declare the global variable with the path to task `state` file:

```
var stateFile = fmt.Sprintf("%s/%s", os.TempDir(), "state.json")
```

In the `handle update` function, just after updating the task state, save it to the file:

```
stateJSON, _ := json.Marshal(tasksState)
ioutil.WriteFile(stateFile, stateJSON, 0644)
```

We will load the previous state in the dedicated function and that should be called after the `frameworkId` is stored in the framework info:

```
func reconcile() {
        oldState, err := ioutil.ReadFile(stateFile)
        if err == nil {
                json.Unmarshal(oldState, &tasksState)
        }
var oldTasks []*Call_Reconcile_Task
maxID := 0
for _, t := range tasksState {
        oldTasks = append(oldTasks, &Call_Reconcile_Task{
                TaskId: t.TaskId,
                AgentId: t.AgentId,
        })
        numericID, err := strconv.Atoi(t.TaskId.GetValue())
        if err == nil && numericID > maxID {
                maxID = numericID
        }
```

```
    }
    atomic.StoreUint64(&taskID, uint64(maxID))
    call(&Call{
        Type: Call_RECONCILE.Enum(),
        Reconcile: &Call_Reconcile{Tasks: oldTasks},
    })
}
```

In this function, we do more than just load the task state. We find the maximum task ID, just to start a counter with the next unused value, but more importantly, we also send a reconcile message to Mesos.

How it works...

Reconciliation allows the framework to ask Mesos about the state of its tasks. When Mesos gets a list of task IDs, it will send update events for every listed task. This allows frameworks to get information about their tasks after disconnection, for example after the framework restarts. It's good practice to periodically reconcile all tasks. It's a way to synchronize the state of all framework's tasks, just in case some events were dropped.

5
Managing Containers

In this chapter, you will learn about containers and isolators and the manner in which they can be used to provide a secure and efficient environment for running applications on Mesos.

The following are the topics covered in the chapter:

- Enabling the Mesos containerizer
- Enabling POSIX isolators
- Enabling the POSIX disk isolator
- Configuring the shared filesystem isolator
- Configuring cgroup isolators
- Configuring the port mapping network isolator
- Configuring Docker image support for the Mesos containerizer
- Using the Docker containerizer
- Running an image from a private repository
- Using the container network interface
- Monitoring containers with Sysdig

Introduction

In 2006, engineers from Google started working on enabling the running of applications in separated environments on the Linux kernel. This was not a new approach. Similar techniques were used in BSD Jails and Solaris Zones. In 2013, Docker became publicly available. The container revolution started and Docker became a synonymous with container. For developers, containerization meant that they could pack their application with all dependencies and it would run exactly the same as on their machines as it would on their machines. For admins, containers meant less configuration coupling between the machine and applications because applications contained definitions for all dependencies. In the long run, containers are significantly cheaper than virtual machines.

Enabling the Mesos containerizer

In this recipe, you will learn how to enable the Mesos containerizer. The Mesos containerizer (a.k.a. the unified containerizer) is the default way of running containers on Mesos. It can support multiple types of isolation, providing the ability to configure process isolation to match system requirements. Starting Mesos version 1.0, container images in Docker and AppC formats are supported.

Getting ready

You need to have Mesos up and running. See the recipes of `Chapter 1`, *Getting Started with Apache Mesos* to get more information.

How to do it...

The Mesos containerizer is enabled by default. To make it explicit, run the following command:

```
echo 'mesos' > /etc/mesos-slave/containerizers
```

How it works...

The Mesos agent reads the list of enabled containerizers and enables matching implementations. If you want to run a container that is not supported by a particular agent, the task won't start. The Mesos containerizer interacts with the native kernel's `cgroups` mechanism and does not provide features like Docker. It's dedicated to just isolating processes and limiting the resources they are using. It's the best option for running statically-linked applications with minimal dependencies such as programs written in Go.

Caution: `etc/mesos-slave/isolation` takes a comma-delimited list of isolators. The following examples will overwrite the content of the file to make the code simpler to present. Nothing stops you from mixing and matching the required values.For example:

```
posix/cpu,posix/mem,disk/du
```

Enabling POSIX isolators

In this recipe, you will learn the difference between POSIX isolators and containers. POSIX isolators are very basic and should not be used in production.

Getting ready

You need to have Mesos up and running. See the recipes of `Chapter 1`, *Getting Started with Apache Mesos* to get more information.

How to do it....

POSIX isolators are enabled by default for CPU and memory. To make this explicit, use:

```
echo "posix/cpu,posix/mem" > /etc/mesos-slave/isolation
```

How it works...

POSIX isolators are not real isolators. They do not create proper containers that allow them to separate a process from the rest of the system using Linux kernel features. Instead, you should run tasks in separated processes and periodically check the resources they are using but do not limit them.

Enabling the POSIX disk isolator

The POSIX disk isolator does not perform isolation like a POSIX isolator. It monitors and limits resources by killing tasks that exceed a given quota. In this recipe, you will learn how to limit applications to the size of each sandbox.

Getting ready

You need to have Mesos up and running. See the recipes of Chapter 1, *Getting Started with Apache Mesos* to get more information.

How to do it...

To enable the POSIX disk isolator, we need to append disk/du to the isolators list:

```
echo "disk/du" > /etc/mesos-slave/isolation
```

This will enable periodic checking of the sandbox size. To enforce a kill policy on tasks that reach their limit, we need to explicitly turn it on:

```
touch /etc/mesos-slave/enforce_container_disk_quota
```

Mesos will now check all sandbox sizes with du and kill one if it uses more disk space than the allocated limit. To change this interval to 5 minutes, use following code:

```
echo "5mins" > /etc/mesos-slave/container_disk_watch_interval
```

How it works...

Similar to other POSIX isolators, the disk isolator does not perform the real separation of disk resources between tasks. It periodically checks the size of a sandbox. It's worth mentioning that processes are still able to create files outside their sandboxes and these files won't count toward the disk limit. Checking more frequently with a lower time interval could damage performance; on the other hand, setting too big a value will cause some tasks to take many more resources and reduce the space available for other tasks. A good starting point would be 15 or 30 seconds. This shouldn't have a negative impact on performance but still could be dangerous. 15 seconds is enough time to generate gigabytes of logs so before you do it, ensure all applications send their logs to some centralized system and do not write logs into `stdout` or `stderr`.

Configuring the shared filesystem isolator

In this recipe, you will learn how to enable the `SharedFilesystem` isolator. This isolator allows us to mount a given directory inside a sandbox so that tasks will not interact with other processes' files.

Getting ready

You need to have Mesos up and running. See the recipes of `Chapter 1`, *Getting Started with Apache Mesos* to get more information.

How to do it...

To enable `SharedFilesystem`, we need to define the host path (the path of the shared filesystem) and where it should be mounted in the container. In the following example, we are mounting `/tmp` path under `.local/tmp`:

```
cat <<EOF > /etc/mesos-slave/default_container_info
{
  "type": "MESOS",
  "volumes": [
    {
      "host_path": ".local/tmp",
      "container_path": "/tmp",
```

```
        "mode": "RW"
      }
    ]
  }
EOF
```

How it works...

The `SharedFilesystem` isolator allows us to exclude some paths from the shared filesystem and keep them locally inside the sandbox. This prevents us overwriting data and its extremely useful for the `tmp` directory as well as the user's home directory. Imagine applications that were written and deployed on dedicated servers or virtual machines; when we want them to run on a shared machine, multiple instances of one application could run on one node at the same time. If the application stores some temporary directory without using a system call to generate a unique directory each time, we could end up with a situation where two instances will overwrite the same file. Another reason to enable this isolator is to delete all the application's temporary data with its sandbox. Imagine a situation where an application uses a unique directory for every instance, but when it gets killed, this data persists on the system until the next reboot.

The path we want to mimic must exist and can't be a parent directory of a Mesos sandbox. So, for example, if we keep Mesos metadata in `/tmp` (which is not recommended but useful when we do not use persistent storage and want reboot to reset agent metadata) we can't make `map /tmp`.

Configuring cgroup isolators

In this recipe, you will learn how to create a container with `cgroups`, that is, real resource isolation at the kernel level.

Getting ready

You need to have Mesos up and running. See the recipes of `Chapter 1`, *Getting Started with Apache Mesos* to get more information.

How to do it...

`cgroups` isolators are enabled in the same manner as POSIX. We need to put a comma-separated list of isolators into the configuration file:

```
echo "cgroups/cpu,cgroups/mem,namespaces/pid" > /etc/mesos-slave/isolation
```

By default, Mesos uses soft CPU limits. This means a process will get at least the resources it was allocated but there is a huge chance that it will use more CPU time when doing more intensive operations. To change this behavior, create this file:

```
touch /etc/mesos-slave/cgroups_enable_cfs
```

How it works...

`cgroup` is a Linux mechanism for limiting and isolating processes. `cgroup` isolation creates a real container for our application. This means when it tries to allocate more memory than declared, it will be killed with an **Out Of Memory (OOM)** error. The reason why the task was killed is available in a `TaskStatus.Reason` message sent to the framework. For example, the reason for killing tasks with OOM looks like this:

```
Memory limit exceeded: Requested: 32MB Maximum Used: 32MB MEMORY
STATISTICS: cache 4096 rss 33550336 rss_huge 0 mapped_file 0 dirty 4096
writeback 0 pgpgin 9845 pgpgout 1653 pgfault 12174 pgmajfault 1
inactive_anon 0 active_anon 33550336 inactive_file 4096 active_file 0
unevictable 0 hierarchical_memory_limit 33554432 total_cache 4096 total_rss
33550336 total_rss_huge 0 total_mapped_file 0 total_dirty 4096
total_writeback 0 total_pgpgin 9845 total_pgpgout 1653 total_pgfault 12174
total_pgmajfault 1 total_inactive_anon 0 total_active_anon 33550336
total_inactive_file 4096 total_active_file 0 total_unevictable 0
```

When `cgroups` CFS is enabled, computation time will be limited. It's recommended to run it using hard limits on the system, especially when performing performance tests. It's a common mistake to test applications on a dedicated agent with soft limits and then observe performance degradation in production where it shares agents with other processes. The namespace isolator ensures our process won't get information about other processes running on the system.

Although Docker is considered THE standard for containerization, it utilizes the same kernel mechanism as `cgroup` isolators. Docker brings more features but also comes with some overhead. Before stepping into Docker containers, make sure you really need the features that come with them. Maybe `cgroups` containers will be enough instead. `cgroups` containers are useful when deploying applications with the same organization-wide setup or without system dependencies.

Configuring the port mapping network isolator

In this recipe, you will learn how to enable network isolation, which will enable per container network statistics and allow port mapping.

Getting ready

The Mesos port mapping network isolator requires Linux kernel version 3.15 or later. To build and run it, the following dependencies must be installed on the system:

```
apt-get install libnl-3-dev libnl-3-200 iproute
```

It also requires building Mesos from source with the following configuration flag enabled:

```
./configure --with-network-isolator
```

How to do it...

To enable the network isolator, you need to put `network/port_mapping` in `/etc/mesos-slave/isolation`:

```
echo "network/port_mapping" > /etc/mesos-slave/isolation
```

How it works...

The Mesos port mapping network isolator isolates ports used by container, so it will prevent applications from binding to ports that are not declared to them. It also enables network statistics in the `/monitor/statistics` agent endpoint. Because it requires a specific Linux kernel version and additional libraries, it's not enabled with default compilation and needs to be explicitly enabled. Under the hood, this isolator is using network namespace. This is the part of the Linux kernel that allows virtualization of the network. This allows the creation of virtual devices, ports, nets, and routes and with this, tools control traffic.

Configuring Docker image support for the Mesos containerizer

In this recipe, you will learn how to configure Mesos to run Docker images with the Mesos containerizer. A Docker image is a file that specifies a container. From version 1.0 on, Mesos understands this format and can create a container using declared isolators that will run a given image. It's worth mentioning that not all features of Docker are supported and if you need full Docker support, take a look at the Docker containerizer.

Getting ready

You need to have Mesos up and running. See the recipes of Chapter 1, *Getting Started with Apache Mesos* to get more information.

How to do it...

Enable Docker image support by setting:

```
echo 'docker' > /etc/mesos-slave/image_providers
```

Add `filesystem` and Docker isolation. This is required because Docker changes ownership of files, which can be done only with a `filesystem` isolator:

```
echo 'filesystem/linux,docker/runtime' > /etc/mesos-slave/isolation
```

How it works...

A Mesos agent reads configuration from the file and from enabled, defined image providers. Currently, there are only Docker and AppC image definition. Because Docker requires specific isolation, we need to enable it as well.

When a Mesos agent gets a request to run a Docker image, instead of calling Docker daemon, it will run the container by itself. Under the hood, Docker is just a set of scripts that interacts with the Linux kernel to run a defined image. The Mesos containerizer is just a different implementation of Docker. Although Mesos can read and run Docker images, there could be some implementation details that differ or even features that are not implemented (for example, port mappings), so it's recommended to stick with one method of running Docker images in the whole development process.

Using the Docker containerizer

In this recipe, you will learn how to enable and run Docker images with a Docker containerizer. What this means is instead of using the Mesos implementation of standard Docker, we will use the Docker daemon to run images.

These days, Docker is the standard for containerization. Mesos supports two ways of launching Docker images. The first implemented was Docker containerizer, which is just a wrapper for the Docker daemon. Mesos does not launch containers itself. Instead, it asks the Docker daemon to do it. When a container is launched, Mesos monitors its state and bypasses framework commands (for example, `kill`) to the Docker daemon.

There is a second way of running Docker images, introduced in Mesos 1.0. It uses the Mesos containerizer to launch Docker images. Using this approach, no Docker installation is required and Mesos performs all the operations itself.

Getting ready

Install Docker on all agents:

```
sudo apt-key adv --keyserver hkp://p80.pool.sks-keyservers.net:80 --recv-
keys 58118E89F3A912897C070ADBF76221572C52609D
echo "deb https://apt.dockerproject.org/repo ubuntu-xenial main" | sudo tee
/etc/apt/sources.list.d/docker.list
sudo apt-get update
sudo apt-get install -y docker-engine
```

Alternatively, you can use the script provided by Docker:

```
curl -fsSL https://get.docker.com/ | sh
```

Full documentation can be found at `https://docs.docker.com/engine/installation/`.

How to do it...

Enable the Docker containerizer for Mesos:

```
echo 'docker,mesos' > /etc/mesos-slave/containerizers
```

How it works...

There is huge difference between these two types of containerizers. Using Docker allows you to use the same software as developers use while they're preparing images to be deployed. Minimizing dependencies and iterations with other software is always recommended when deploying mission critical applications in production. The Docker daemon has an established universe of tools to monitor and manage it, while Mesos is still quite fresh.

Running an image from a private repository

A private repository gives you total control over who is able to push and pull images. This improves security by limiting access and keeping a full audit log. With proper configuration of caching and load balancing, a private repository can also speed up deployments.

In this recipe, you will learn how to configure Mesos to use a custom Docker repository with optional authentication. This will enable you to host a private repository inside your organization.

Getting ready

You need to have Docker support enabled; see the *Configuring Docker image support for Mesos containerizer* and *Using Docker containerizer* recipes to get more information.

How to do it...

Create a Docker configuration with the address and credentials of your repository:

```
cat <<EOF > /etc/mesos-slave/docker_config
{
    "auths": {
      "quay.io": {
        "auth": "xXxXxXxXxXx="
      },
      "https://index.docker.io/v1/": {
        "auth": "xXxXxXxXxXx="
      },
      "https://index.example.com": {
        "auth": "XxXxXxXxXxX="
      }
    }
  }
EOF
```

Here, the `auth` token is a `base64` encoded string: `base64(<username>:<password>)`.

How it works...

A Mesos agent will read Docker config at the start and then pass the provided values to the containerizer.

Using container network interface

In this recipe, you will learn how to enable CNI, which is a common interface used by different container runtimes to provide network isolation and configuration for containers.

Getting ready

You need to have Mesos up and running. See the recipes of `Chapter 1`, *Getting Started with Apache Mesos* to get more information.

How to do it...

CNI is enabled by default in Mesos. All we need is to download the plugins we want to use and provide configuration. Create two directories; one for plugins and one for configuration:

```
mkdir -p /etc/mesos-slave/cni/plugins
mkdir -p /etc/mesos-slave/cni/config
```

Then download and un-compress the plugins:

```
wget
https://github.com/containernetworking/cni/releases/download/v0.3.0/cni-v0.
3.0.tgz
tar xvf cni-v0.3.0.tgz -C /etc/mesos-slave/cni/plugins
```

Write simple config that will create a bridged subnetwork with the IP range `172.16.28.0/24` and the ability to talk with external networks through NAT:

```
cat << EOF > /etc/mesos-slave/cni/config/test.json
{
 "name": "test",
 "type": "bridge",
 "bridge": "mesos-cni-test0",
 "isGateway": true,
 "ipMasq": true,
 "ipam": {
     "type": "host-local",
     "subnet": "172.16.28.0/24",
     "routes": [
     { "dst":
     "0.0.0.0/0" }
     ]
   }
 }
EOF
```

This configuration tells the CNI plugin to create a bridge network called `mesos-cni-test0` and to link it with a name test that will be available for Mesos containers. This network is a gateway so it allows us to send packages outside of the network to all destinations.

How it works...

CNI is a project focused on building pluggable networking solutions for the container ecosystem on Linux. It's supported by rkt, Mesos, Kubernetes, and other container runtimes. With CNI, we can create subnets for specific groups of applications and give each container an individual IP. In this recipe, we defined a subnet for containers called `test`. This network is created when needed. When we run tasks attached to this network and then run `ifconfig`, we should see our network with other interfaces.

CNI allows us to provide custom plugins from third-party software such as Project Calico. This allows us to expose a container's IP outside of the agent machine, allowing us to enhance security and use a regular network stack as we will use with VMs.

Monitoring containers with Sysdig

In this recipe, you will learn how to get events from containers with Sysdig, a tool for collecting system events. It supports containers from both Docker and Mesos and it integrates with Mesos, Marathon, and Kubernetes, matching containers with task, application, or pod. With Sysdig, you can easily detect what is wrong with the container by looking at its events.

Getting ready

You need to have Mesos up and running. See the recipes of `Chapter 1`, *Getting Started with Apache Mesos* to get more information.

How to do it...

Install Sysdig on all agents:

```
curl -s https://s3.amazonaws.com/download.draios.com/DRAIOS-GPG-KEY.public
| apt-key add -
 curl -s -o /etc/apt/sources.list.d/draios.list
http://download.draios.com/stable/deb/draios.list
 apt-get update
apt-get -y install linux-headers-$(uname -r)
apt-get -y install sysdig
```

Then log in to an interesting agent and run:

```
csysdig -m http://<MESOS_IP>:<MESOS_PORT> -pm mesos.task.id!=''
```

For example, if your Mesos is running on host 10.10.10.10:5050, the command will look like this:

```
csysdig -m http://10.10.10.10:5050,http://10.10.10.10:8080 -pm
mesos.task.id!=''
```

This is the Sysdig screen for an agent with two running executors:

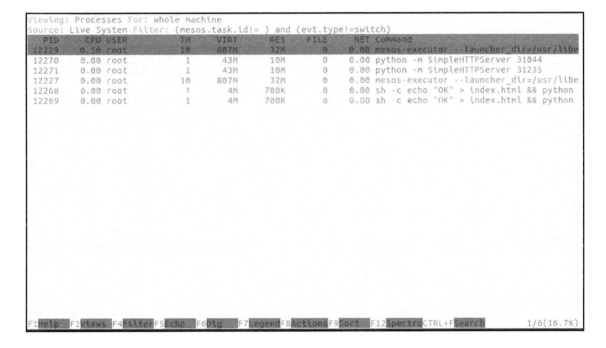

This will show you all tasks with non-empty Mesos task ID; basically all processes managed by Mesos. On servers with tens of tasks on each agent, it will be easier to change view to one that allows better filtering, for example Mesos tasks. In this view, we can navigate to an interesting container and capture what happens inside it. This is the `Sysdig` screen showing the various events for the processes:

```
Viewing: sysdig output For: proc.pid=12271           PAUSED
Source: Live System Filter: (mesos.task.id!= ) and ((evt.type!=switch) and proc.pid=12271)

172813 12:53:25.155993204 1 python (12271) > fstat fd=5(<f>/var/lib/mesos/slaves/e1119c1a-1812-4ecc-af95-
172814 12:53:25.155995440 1 python (12271) < fstat res=0
172815 12:53:25.156009524 1 python (12271) > sendto fd=4(<4t>10.10.10.10:46644->10.10.10.10:31235) size=1
172816 12:53:25.156020550 1 python (12271) < sendto res=19 data=Content-Length: 3..
172818 12:53:25.156051186 1 python (12271) > sendto fd=4(<4t>10.10.10.10:46644->10.10.10.10:31235) size=4
172819 12:53:25.156062779 1 python (12271) < sendto res=46 data=Last-Modified: Wed, 05 Oct 2016 12:22:24
172820 12:53:25.156075510 1 python (12271) > sendto fd=4(<4t>10.10.10.10:46644->10.10.10.10:31235) size=2
172821 12:53:25.156084987 1 python (12271) < sendto res=2 data=..
172822 12:53:25.156100257 1 python (12271) > fstat fd=5(<f>/var/lib/mesos/slaves/e1119c1a-1812-4ecc-af95-
172823 12:53:25.156101461 1 python (12271) < fstat res=0
172824 12:53:25.156103100 1 python (12271) > read fd=5(<f>/var/lib/mesos/slaves/e1119c1a-1812-4ecc-af95-6
172825 12:53:25.156108052 1 python (12271) < read res=3 data=OK.
172826 12:53:25.156109121 1 python (12271) > read fd=5(<f>/var/lib/mesos/slaves/e1119c1a-1812-4ecc-af95-6
172827 12:53:25.156110001 1 python (12271) < read res=0 data=
172828 12:53:25.156122874 1 python (12271) > sendto fd=4(<4t>10.10.10.10:46644->10.10.10.10:31235) size=3
172829 12:53:25.156250926 1 python (12271) < sendto res=3 data=OK.
172830 12:53:25.156258918 1 python (12271) > read fd=5(<f>/var/lib/mesos/slaves/e1119c1a-1812-4ecc-af95-6
172831 12:53:25.156260804 1 python (12271) < read res=0 data=
172832 12:53:25.156269336 1 python (12271) > close fd=5(<f>/var/lib/mesos/slaves/e1119c1a-1812-4ecc-af95-
172833 12:53:25.156271681 1 python (12271) < close res=0
172834 12:53:25.156326594 1 python (12271) > shutdown fd=4(<4t>10.10.10.10:46644->10.10.10.10:31235) how=
172835 12:53:25.156342081 1 python (12271) < shutdown res=0
172837 12:53:25.156355231 1 python (12271) > close fd=4(<4t>10.10.10.10:46644->10.10.10.10:31235)
172838 12:53:25.156356613 1 python (12271) < close res=0
172839 12:53:25.156388645 1 python (12271) > select
179255 12:53:25.657125111 1 python (12271) < select res=0
179256 12:53:25.657194499 1 python (12271) > select
F1Help  F2View As CTRL+FSearchp Pause BakBack  c Clear CTRL+GGoto            119/146(100.0%)
```

How it works...

Sysdig installs an event probe inside the kernel, captures events, and sends them to an event handler, which is responsible for passing them to the user. The event probe uses the kernel trace system to get information about syscalls. All events are copied to a shared buffer and then consumed by the handler. Because the probe resists in kernel space, it's critical to make it as easy as possible to provide the best performance. On the other hand, the handler lives in user space, which means it can be frozen by a kernel when other processes require system time. We can lose some information, but the handler won't decrease system performance. The handler is responsible for reading raw events from the probe and presenting them to the user in human-readable format.

When the handler gets information about Mesos, Marathon, or Kubernetes endpoints, it will gather information from them and enhance the container's data with information obtained from their runtimes.

6

Deploying PaaS with Marathon

In this chapter, you will learn how to install and configure Marathon and other tools required to set up private PaaS.

This chapter covers the following recipes:

- Installing and configuring Marathon
- Monitoring Marathon
- Launching an application
- Launching a Docker container
- Setting up discovery `serviceEnabling SSLEnabling` basic authentication
- Using the custom authentication plugin
- Tuning Marathon

Introduction

Platform as a Service (**PaaS**) is a foundation of modern IT. Containers and orchestrators allow a developer to easily develop and deploy services without worrying about system dependencies and resources. Marathon is an example of a container orchestrator focused on creating private PaaS. Marathon works as a Mesos framework and presents REST APIs for deploying long-running jobs in containers. Marathon's main competitors are Apache Aurora, a battle-tested Mesos framework developed by Twitter, and Kubernetes, both a standalone and a Mesos framework focused on the **Google Infrastructure For Everyone Else** (**GIFFE**) project, which was started in 2014 by Google and has now been adopted by other companies.

Installing and configuring Marathon

Marathon installation is pretty straightforward. Once you have Mesos running, you only need to install one deb and provide the Mesos master location and ZooKeeper to keep a state. In this recipe, you will learn how to set up Marathon.

Getting ready

You need to have Mesos up and running. See `Chapter 1`, *Getting Started with Apache Mesos* for more information.

How to do it...

1. First add Mesosphere repositories to your system. You can skip this step if you installed Mesos from the Mesosphere repositories:

    ```
    apt-key adv --keyserver keyserver.ubuntu.com --recv E56151BF
    DISTRO=$(lsb_release -is | tr '[:upper:]' '[:lower:]')
    CODENAME=$(lsb_release -cs)
    echo "deb http://repos.mesosphere.com/${DISTRO} ${CODENAME} main" >
    /etc/apt/sources.list.d/mesosphere.list
    ```

2. Once all the repositories are added, refresh their state and `install marathon`:

    ```
    apt-get -y update
    apt-get -y install marathon
    ```

3. After installing, we need to provide two important areas of information, where is Mesos and where is the stored data:

    ```
    cat << EOF > /etc/default/marathon
    MARATHON_MASTER=zk://10.10.10.10:2181/mesos
    MARATHON_ZK=zk://10.10.10.10:2181/marathon
    EOF
    ```

4. When the ZooKeeper cluster has more nodes, each node should be specified and separated by a comma in the same manner as in the Mesos configuration.

5. To communicate with Mesos, Marathon requires the Mesos native library. If it's not stored in the default location then, `MESOS_NATIVE_JAVA_LIBRARY` should be set:

```
Echo MESOS_NATIVE_JAVA_LIBRARY=/usr/lib/libmesos.so >>
/etc/default/marathon
```

How it works...

Marathon uses the deprecated Mesos native library to communicate with Mesos. That's why it requires ZooKeeper as a way to detect the Mesos leader. Marathon, similar to Mesos, uses ZooKeeper to elect the leader. When the leader is elected, other Marathon nodes are in standby mode waiting for a new election. Marathon uses ZooKeeper to keep the entire state of running applications, groups, tasks, and pending deployments. It's a good idea to run Marathon on a separate ZooKeeper cluster, which can be installed on Marathon masters.

Monitoring Marathon

Marathon can send logs and metrics to dedicated systems, such as Kibana for logs and Graphite for metrics. To enable them, we need to change the configuration. In this recipe, you will learn how to collect logs and metrics from Marathon.

Getting ready

Before you start, ensure Marathon is up and running. In this recipe, we will assume you have a running Graphite instance at `http://graphite.readthedocs.io/en/latest/insta ll.html`.

How to do it...

In the following example, we assume Graphite is reachable at `graphite.local` at port `2003` and accepts TCP packages. The following configuration instructs Marathon to send metrics every 30 seconds and to prefix them with `marathon`:

```
cat << EOF >> /etc/default/marathon
MARATHON_REPORTER_GRAPHITE=tcp://graphite.local:2003?prefix=marathon&interv
al=30
EOF
```

Enabling logging with `logstash` is similar. Let's assume `logstash` reads incoming logs at `logstash.local` at port 5000:

```
cat << EOF >> /etc/default/marathon
MARATHON_LOGSTASH=udp://logstash.local:5000
EOF
```

How it works...

Marathon exposes its metrics at the `/metrics` endpoint. By enabling export to Graphite, we make it to push metrics every given time. The interval should be correlated with the Graphite setting to ensure collected data is continuous (when the interval is too big, points won't be connected and some metric aggregations will not work). A prefix is added at the beginning of each metric. In our example, all metrics can be found in the `marathon` subtree.

By default, Marathon logs to `stdout` and `syslog`. At any given moment, you can view your logs with the following:

```
journalctl -f -u marathon or in /var/log/syslog
```

Launching an application

In this recipe, you will learn how to launch an application using the Marathon API. We will create our first application using the API and then write a simple Python script to obtain information about where it has been deployed. Marathon provides a REST API that allows us to easily wire it with CI/CD systems using a simple script.

Getting ready

Before you start, ensure Marathon is up and running.

How to do it...

When you log in to Marathon, you can manually click to deploy an application. The Marathon UI is great, but limited to performing only basic deployments. In the following examples, you will see how to interact with Marathon using its API. This will enable you to plug in Marathon as a final step of your CI/CD solution.

There are two types of applications: native and Docker.

1. The first example will show how to deploy a simple web server:

```
cat <<EOF > caddy.json
{
  "id": "web/server",
  "cmd": "echo \"It's working!\" > index.html &&
  ./caddy_linux_amd64 -port
$PORT0",
  "cpus": 1.0,
  "mem": 32,
  "disk": 10,
  "instances": 1,
  "healthChecks": [
    {
    "path": "/",
    "protocol": "HTTP",
    "portIndex": 0,
    "gracePeriodSeconds": 1,
    "intervalSeconds": 5,
    "timeoutSeconds": 20,
    "maxConsecutiveFailures": 3,
    "ignoreHttp1xx": false
    }
  ],
  "labels": {
    "label": "value"
  },
  "portDefinitions": [
    {
    "protocol": "tcp",
    "labels": {
        "label": "http"
      }
    }
  ],
    "fetch": [
    {
    "uri":
"https://github.com/mholt/caddy/releases/download/v0.9.3/caddy_linu
x_amd64.tar.gz",
    "extract": true,
    "executable": false,
    "cache": false
    }
  ]
}
```

```
EOF
curl -H "Content-Type: application/json" -X POST --data @caddy.json
10.10.10.10:8080/v2/apps
```

2. After a while, we can see in the Marathon UI that a new application appears. We can click through it and get its address, but we can do the same with the API:

   ```
   curl 10.10.10.10:8080/v2/apps/web/server?embed=apps.tasks | python
   -m json.tool
   ```

3. With a simple one-liner, we can extract all host:[ports] of running instances:

   ```
   curl 10.10.10.10:8080/v2/apps/web/server?embed=apps.tasks | python
   -c 'import sys, json; print [task["host"] + ":" +
   str(task["ports"]) for task in
   json.load(sys.stdin)["app"]["tasks"]];'
   ```

How it works...

In the preceding example, we defined an application called web/server. This name is meaningful because it means an application server will be placed in a web group. If you look carefully in the UI, you will notice that our application is presented as a server in the web directory. This feature is called groups. We can group an application into logical structures the same as directories by splitting the ID with /. It's your decision as to how you will use groups. They are not obligatory but help keep applications in order, especially when their numbers increase. When somebody deletes a web group, they will also kill our application.

An application definition is translated into a Mesos Task request in the same way that when we developed our framework. When Marathon starts a task, a bunch of environment variables are set in the task runtime:

- MARATHON_APP_ID
- MARATHON_APP_VERSION
- MARATHON_APP_DOCKER_IMAGE
- MARATHON_APP_RESOURCE_CPUS
- MARATHON_APP_RESOURCE_MEM
- MARATHON_APP_RESOURCE_DISK
- MARATHON_APP_LABELS

- MARATHON_APP_LABEL_NAME
- MESOS_TASK_ID
- MESOS_SANDBOX
- PORTS: comma-separated list of assigned host ports

If tasks have allocated ports, their numbers are also put in the variables named PORT<port number>, where port indexation starts from 0. So the first defined port appears in $PORT0, the second in $PORT1, and so on. Marathon gives us many other features, such as variable interpolation, so we can use variables, such as $PORT0, that define the environment where the application is spawned.

The important part of an application definition involves health checks. In a distributed world, it's critical to detect tasks that are running but not working in the way we expect. When a health check fails, Marathon can kill a broken instance and spawn a new one. The port definition section allows us to define ports of our application and give each port its label, similar to application labels where we can store some metadata used by other software. When the specified port is 0, then Mesos will assign a random port. If a user wants to select a specific port (which is not recommended), then they should add requirePorts: true in the application definition.

Launching a Docker container

In this recipe, you will learn how to launch a Docker container using the Marathon API. Marathon, as with most Mesos frameworks, is able to run Docker containers. This is extremely useful in a private PaaS because developers are able to ship their machines into production with one simple click without worrying about server configuration or asking admins for help.

Getting ready

Before you start, ensure Marathon is up and running and Mesos has enabled Docker support. You can find more information in Chapter 5, *Managing Containers*.

How to do it...

The operation is similar to running a command. The main difference is that we need to pass the Docker image description and its configuration such as ports, variables, and optional Docker parameters. Remember to enable Docker support on Mesos agents before proceeding.

The application definition could look as follows:

```
{
  "id": "/web/server",
  "cpus": 1.0,
  "mem": 64,
  "disk": 0,
  "instances": 1,
  "container": {
    "type": "DOCKER",
    "volumes": [],
    "docker": {
      "image": "yobasystems/alpine-caddy",
      "network": "BRIDGE",
      "portMappings": [
        {
          "containerPort": 2015,
          "hostPort": 0,
          "protocol": "tcp",
          "name": "http",
          "labels": {}
        }
      ],
      "privileged": false,
      "parameters": [],
      "forcePullImage": false
    }
  },
  "healthChecks": [
  {
      "path": "/",
      "protocol": "HTTP",
      "portIndex": 0,
      "gracePeriodSeconds": 300,
      "intervalSeconds": 60,
      "timeoutSeconds": 20,
      "maxConsecutiveFailures": 3,
      "ignoreHttp1xx": false
    }
  ],
```

```
    "portDefinitions": [
      {
        "port": 10001,
        "protocol": "tcp",
        "labels": {}
      }
    ]
  }
```

The steps to deploy an application are the same for Docker as they are for a command.

How it works...

Marathon translates the application definition to a Mesos Protobuf object, which has a dedicated message format for handling Docker containers. Marathon also supports the native Mesos containerizer. To run a Docker image without Docker installed, ensure that the support for the native containerizer is enabled and change `container.type` from `DOCKER` to `MESOS`. You can also run Docker containers in `HOST` network mode. To do this, simply change `BRIDGE` to `HOST` and delete the port mapping section. Remember that without port mappings, your container should bind to ports provided by Mesos (for example, `$PORT0`).

 Keep in mind that the Mesos containerizer is still under heavy development and not all Docker features are available (for example, a bridged networking), and in some cases it could behave differently.

Setting up the discovery service

One of the major problems with running services in a shared environment is the network. How can we make sure services can talk to each other while they could be spawned on different machines and ports? In this recipe, you will learn how to run the discovery service for Marathon to enable services to find each other and we will use the proxy approach with Traefik.

Getting ready

Before you start, ensure Marathon is up and running.

How to do it...

This solution is recommended for small and medium sized clusters with fewer than hundreds of services and fewer than thousands of instances with moderate traffic. With bigger clusters, you will probably need a different approach than a central proxy, such as consul, where you can use allegro/marathon-consul.

Before we start to think about where the proxy should be placed, remember that the more nodes you have, the more proxies you will need. On the other hand, each proxy will query Marathon so it will decrease performance. In this example, we will show how to configure the proxy on one server, which can also be scaled up and configured on more servers.

First, download Traefik:

```
wget https://github.com/containous/traefik/releases/download/v1.0.3/traefik
-O /usr/bin/traefik
chmod +x /usr/bin/traefik
```

Then create a configuration file. We assume Marathon is available at `10.10.10.10:8080`. Remember to change it to your configuration. If you have multiple Marathon instances, add all of them, separating them with a comma. For example, `http://10.10.10.10:8080,127.0.0.1:8080`:

```
mkdir -p /etc/traefik
cat <<EOF > /etc/traefik/traefik.toml
[web]
address = ":8088"
[marathon]
endpoint = "http://10.10.10.10:8080"
watch = true
domain = "marathon"
exposedByDefault = true
groupsAsSubDomains = true
EOF
```

In the preceding configuration, we ask Traefik to start its API on port 8080. Then we declare to use Marathon as a source of services. By default, Traefik will use the first port of service. We set it to expose all applications by default and to generate their names using `groups` as a subdomain, setting the default domain to `marathon` so our application will be available as `<name>.<group>.marathon`, for example `web.server.marathon`.

Next, we need to make sure Traefik will be supervised by the system:

```
cat <<EOF > /etc/systemd/system/traefik.service
[Unit]
Description=Traefik
Wants=network-online.target
After=network.target network-online.target
[Service]
Restart=on-failure
ExecStart=/usr/bin/traefik
[Install]
WantedBy=multi-user.target
EOF
```

Finally, start Traefik:

```
service traefik start
```

Check it's working by visiting port 8088. You can also query your service with curl:

```
curl -H Host:web.server.marathon http://127.0.0.1
```

Setting headers for every request and the IP of Traefik is error-prone. Let's create the resolve rule so all requests for the Marathon domain will be passed to our Traefik instance.

To do this, we need to handle the wildcard DNS queries. There is a program that can handle that: dnsmasq. We need to install and configure it to resolve all Marathon domains to our Traefik instance:

```
apt-get install dnsmasq
cat << EOF > /etc/dnsmasq.conf
address=/marathon/10.10.10.10
EOF
service dnsmasq restart
```

With the preceding configuration, all requests that end with marathon will be resolved to 10.10.10.10. This operation should be repeated on all hosts that will interact with Marathon applications.

To check if it's working, try to connect with one of your services:

```
curl web.server.marathon
```

How it works...

Traefik is a load balancer, a.k.a. proxy, working on layer 7. It works on a very simple concept that has been around since Apache and PHP. Traefik parses HTTP requests and passes them to matching services. We can achieve similar functionality with Apache, nginx, or HAProxy, but only Traefik comes with built-in Marathon support. What's more, it can integrate with Mesos so we are not tied to Marathon and can use it to integrate services between different Mesos frameworks.

Enabling SSL

In this recipe, you will learn how to enable SSL for Marathon to protect eavesdropping on Marathon communication.

Getting ready

First, we need to create a place for our Java keystore:

```
mkdir -p /etc/marathon/ssl
cd /etc/marathon/ssl
```

Then, put the keystore password into the environment variable. We will need it later:

```
export MARATHON_SSL_KEYSTORE_PASSWORD=jks_pass
```

Generate the keystore. In this example, we will use self-signed certificates but if you can issue an organization-wide trusted certificate, it would be better to use that. With self-signed certificates, most browsers will mark the Marathon UI and API as dangerous and there is a chance that somebody will create a man-in-the-middle attack:

```
keytool -keystore marathon.jks -deststorepass
$MARATHON_SSL_KEYSTORE_PASSWORD -alias marathon -genkey -keyalg RSA
```

How to do it...

Finally, save the Marathon keystore configuration:

```
cat << EOF > /etc/default/marathon
MARATHON_SSL_KEYSTORE_PATH=/etc/marathon/ssl/marathon.jks
MARATHON_SSL_KEYSTORE_PASSWORD=$MARATHON_SSL_KEYSTORE_PASSWORD
EOF
```

```
Restart marathon and check if SSL is working
Service marathon restart
curl -k https://localhost:8443/ping
```

How it works...

Marathon in written in Scala. As a web server, it uses Chaos, a lightweight framework for writing REST services in Scala. Underneath, Chaos uses Jetty and is responsible for creating endpoints. When Marathon sees SSL configuration, it passes credentials and paths to keystores to Chaos so it can open SSL endpoints.

Enable encryption before turning on authentication.

Enabling basic access authentication

In this recipe, you will learn how to enable HTTP basic authentication to limit a user who can access the Marathon API.

Getting ready

Before you start, ensure Marathon is up and running. Before applying any authentication, ensure you enabled SSL to protect secrets from eavesdropping.

How to do it...

Update the configuration with credentials:

```
echo MARATHON_HTTP_CREDENTIALS=username:password >> /etc/default/marathon
```

Check the API requires authentication:

```
curl -k https://localhost:8443/ping
```

The preceding command should return a `401 Unauthorized` code, while the following command should work. From now, all interactions with Marathon require passing credentials:

```
curl -k -u username:password https://localhost:8443/ping
```

How it works...

When HTTP credentials are passed to Marathon, it checks HTTP request headers for credentials and compares them with those configured. When no credentials are provided or the provided credentials don't match, it returns a `401` error code.

Passing credentials in plain text is not recommended.

Using a custom authentication plugin

In this recipe, you will learn how to create an authentication plugin that will allow you to perform fine-grained access control.

Getting ready

Before you start, ensure Marathon is up and running. Before applying any authentication, ensure you enabled SSL to protect secrets from eavesdropping.

How to do it...

Plugins need to be written, so we will use a plugin from the Mesosphere example. It's a good base to start with to write a custom plugin. In this recipe, we will work with Marathon 1.3.5.

First, we need to download the plugin code:

```
curl -L
https://github.com/janisz/marathon-example-plugins/archive/1.3.5.tar.gz |
tar -zx
cd marathon-example-plugins-1.3.5
```

The plugin is written in Scala, and to build it we need the **Scala Build Tool** (**SBT**):

```
curl -s https://raw.githubusercontent.com/paulp/sbt-extras/master/sbt > sbt
&& chmod 0755 sbt
```

Now we can build it. This might take some time because we need to download all the dependencies and then compile the code:

```
./sbt pack
```

Built plugins can be found in ./target/pack/lib:

```
mkdir -p /etc/marathon/plugins
mv ./target/pack/lib/auth-plugin_2.11-1.0.jar /etc/marathon/plugins/
cat << EOF > /etc/marathon/plugins/configuration.json
{
    "plugins": {
      "authorization": {
      "plugin": "mesosphere.marathon.plugin.auth.Authorizer",
      "implementation":
"mesosphere.marathon.example.plugin.auth.ExampleAuthorizer"
      },
      "authentication": {
        "plugin": "mesosphere.marathon.plugin.auth.Authenticator",
        "implementation":
"mesosphere.marathon.example.plugin.auth.ExampleAuthenticator",
        "configuration": {
          "users": [
            {
            "user": "dev",
            "password": "dev",
            "permissions": [
            { "allowed": "create", "on": "/dev/" },
            { "allowed": "update", "on": "/dev/" },
            { "allowed": "delete", "on": "/dev/" },
            { "allowed": "view", "on": "/dev/" }
            ]
          },
          {
            "user": "prod",
            "password": "prod",
            "permissions": [
              { "allowed": "create", "on": "/prod/" },
              { "allowed": "update", "on": "/prod/" },
              { "allowed": "delete", "on": "/prod/" },
              { "allowed": "view", "on": "/prod/" }
            ]
          },
```

```
          {
            "user": "admin",
            "password": "admin",
            "permissions": [
              { "allowed": "create", "on": "/" },
              { "allowed": "update", "on": "/" },
              { "allowed": "delete", "on": "/" },
              { "allowed": "view", "on": "/" }
            ]
          }
        ]
      }
    }
  }
}
EOF
mkdir -p /etc/marathon/conf
echo /etc/marathon/plugins > /etc/marathon/conf/plugin_dir
echo /etc/marathon/plugins/configuration.json >
/etc/marathon/conf/plugin_conf
Service marathon restart
```

Authentication should be up and running. If you analyze the code, you will see that nobody has access to the resources endpoints. This can cause web UI to stop working, but the API should be available. We can check it's working by creating applications in different groups and then checking their visibility:

```
cat <<EOF | curl -u admin:admin -X PUT -H "Content-Type: application/json"
-d @- localhost:8080/v2/apps
[
  {
        "id": "python/simple-http-server",
        "cmd": "python -m SimpleHTTPServer $PORT0"
  },
  {
        "id": "dev/python/simple-http-server",
        "cmd": "python -m SimpleHTTPServer $PORT0"
  },
  {
         "id": "prod/python/simple-http-server",
         "cmd": "python -m SimpleHTTPServer $PORT0"
  }
]
EOF
```

Now we can check that authentication really works by querying the `/v2/apps` endpoint. We should see all the applications when we are logged in as admin; while logging in as `prod` or `dev`, we will see only the defined subset. To check what a given user can see, use the following command:

```
curl -u admin:admin localhost:8080/v2/apps | python -c 'import sys, json;
print [app["id"] for app in json.load(sys.stdin)["apps"]];'
```

To log in as another user, change the credentials passed after the `-u` argument.

How it works...

Marathon allows for the creation of extension with plugins. A plugin is just a JAR that is loaded at the start and is enabled. To make it work, Marathon must know where the binaries are stored and how the classes are named to load them properly. The configuration is loaded by Marathon and passed to initialize the method. When a plugin is wired properly, it's called to authenticate apps and groups API operations. If a given user is not allowed to perform a given action, he will get a HTTP 401 error. The main advantage over basic authentication is that we can have multiple users and control their access rights. What's more, we can wire our custom authentication mechanism. The main drawback of this approach is that the authentication plugin is still under development and its interface changes between releases, so we need to update the code for every Marathon release. Another problem with the authentication plugin comes from its implementation. Every operation on an application or a group needs to be authenticated. This means `isAuthorized` is called for every application and every group. This will work smoothly for small clusters with tens of application, but with hundreds of applications, the API will become slow and could negatively impact the performance of Marathon as a whole. If you need fine-grained access control for hundreds of services, it is better to set up a facade between users and Marathon that will do authentication, or split Marathon into many instances dedicated for every user group. They will all be able to share one Mesos cluster.

Tuning Marathon

In this recipe, you will learn how to configure Marathon to improve its performance.

Getting ready

Before you begin, you should capture Marathon metrics to see whether presented actions give the desired effect.

How to do it...

Marathon has many configuration options that could change its performance. It's written in Scala so it runs on JVM, which has even more options.

Most of the default settings are good enough even for big installations. However, there is a small set that should be changed.

You can gain better performance by changing Marathon's JVM options, especially to give it more memory and change the Garbage Collection algorithm. Tuning JVM is out of the scope of this book, so we will show only the basic methods. The following code will set Marathon to use 2 GB of memory and change the Garbage Collector to G1:

```
echo 'JAVA_OPTS=" -mx2g -ms2g -XX:+UseG1GC -XX:MetaspaceSize=100M"' >>
/etc/default/marathon
```

The next thing that has an impact on performance is how many tasks Marathon launches for one offer. If we increase this number, then more tasks will be spawned on one slave in one cycle:

```
mkdir -p /etc/marathon/conf
echo 30 > /etc/marathon/conf/max_tasks_per_offer
```

How it works...

Tuning JVM and Marathon is difficult. It requires good monitoring and great knowledge of the whole setup. The rule of thumb is to avoid a GC full scan and minimize GC collection time. Without modifying the code, the only way to achieve this is to change the JVM settings. Usually, increasing the heap will cause GC to fire less often. On the other hand, when heap is too big, GC pauses could increase because the heap to scan will be bigger. Tuning this parameter requires some experience and usually means testing several different configurations. Overall, Marathon performance consists of several factors such as ZooKeeper performance, and latency and health check counts (remember all HTTP/TCP health checks are performed by the Marathon master). The default settings are good for small installations, but when there are more and more applications, some actions should be taken. The presented changes are low-hanging fruit that can quickly boost Marathon performance.

7
Job Scheduling with Metronome

In this chapter, we will be covering the following recipes:

- Installing and configuring Metronome
- Monitoring Metronome
- Scheduling jobs

Introduction

Metronome is a Mesos framework designed to schedule time-based jobs. It's written by the same company as Marathon and shares code and architecture with Marathon. Marathon and Metronome have very similar setups and options. If Marathon could be considered as an upstart for Mesos, then Metronome is an implementation of a distributed cron. Metronome is part of DCOS but can be installed separately. Metronome is not the only one time-based scheduler in the Mesos world. It's considered as a successor to Chronos, a time-based scheduler with job dependencies and job history and statistics. Chronos was created at AirBnB, but now its development has slowed down and currently only critical issues are solved. A time-based scheduler is implemented in other frameworks, such as Aurora or Singularity.

Installing and configuring Metronome

In this recipe, you will learn how to set up Metronome.

How to do it...

Metronome installation is a bit harder than Marathon. There are no official binary packages for it, so it must be installed from source.

1. First, we need to download the Metronome source code:

```
curl -L https://github.com/dcos/metronome/archive/v0.1.9.tar.gz |
tar -zx
cd metronome-0.1.9
```

2. Metronome is written in Scala and to build it, we need the **Scala Build Tool** (**SBT**):

```
cho "deb https://dl.bintray.com/sbt/debian /" | sudo tee -a
/etc/apt/sources.list.d/sbt.list
sudo apt-key adv --keyserver hkp://keyserver.ubuntu.com:80 --recv
642AC823
sudo apt-get update
sudo apt-get install sbt
```

3. Install the Protocol Buffer compiler:

```
sudo apt-get install protobuf-compiler
```

4. Finally, build and install the package:

```
sbt universal:packageBin
mkdir -p /opt/mesosphere
unzip target/universal/metronome-0.1.9.zip -d /opt/mesosphere
cat <<EOF > /etc/systemd/system/metronome.service
[Unit]
Description=Metronome
Wants=network-online.target
After=network.target network-online.target
[Service]
Restart=on-failure
ExecStart=/opt/mesosphere/metronome-0.1.9/bin/metronome
[Install]
WantedBy=multi-user.target
EOF
```

5. Metronome configurations can be found here:

```
/opt/mesosphere/metronome-0.1.9/conf/application.conf
```

6. This file has embedded documentation comments which is really easy to understand and change. After setting all the required configurations, we can start Metronome:

```
systemctl enable metronome.service
systemctl start metronome.service
```

7. By default, Metronome starts at port 9000. We can check whether it started at:

```
curl http://10.10.10.10:9000/ping
```

8. If everything is configured correctly, it should appear on the Mesos frameworks dashboard.

How it works...

Metronome uses the same code as Marathon to communicate with Mesos. This is native library, based communication, so currently it doesn't support all the Mesos features that are available with the Mesos HTTP API. Metronome also uses ZooKeeper to elect leaders and store information. In this recipe, we built Metronome from source and create a systemd entry about it. When Metronome starts, it reads the configuration from `application.conf`. This text-based file with JSON-like syntax is well documented and describes all Metronome settings.

Monitoring Metronome

In this recipe, you will learn how to collect logs and metrics from Metronome.

How to do it...

By default, Metronome writes logs to `stdout`. Logs are managed by `logback.conf`, where we can define our custom appender, change what is logged, and change log patterns.

For example, we can extend the stacktrace size from the default 10 to 20 lines. To do this, open `/opt/mesosphere/metronome-0.1.9/conf/logback.conf`, find the `STDOUT` appender, and change the following code:

```
<pattern>%coloredLevel %logger{15} -
%message%n%xException{10}</pattern>
```

Change it to the following code:

```
<pattern>%coloredLevel %logger{15} -
%message%n%xException{20}</pattern>
```

before level information to datetime in log.

Now after the service Metronome restart, you can view your logs with:

```
sudo journalctl -f -u metronome
```

Unfortunately, Metronome does not provide bindings for external monitoring services such as Logstash, Graphite, or Datadog. Logs must be aggregated and parsed by other tools. Metrics can be found at `/v1/metrics`. Metrics are JSON objects, so it should be fairly straightforward to read them with the custom Diamond handler.

How it works...

By default, Metronome writes logs to `stdout`. Logs are managed by Logback, which is a common Java/Scala logging interface. Metrics are collected with standard Scala Akka tools, so we can easily get information about an application's health with details about running actors and JVM statistics:

```
http://10.10.10.10:9000/v1/metrics
```

Scheduling jobs

In this recipe, you will learn how to schedule an application to run periodically. We will use the schedule performance tester which, will send results to other services.

How to do it...

First go to `http://webhook.site/`, copy the destination link, and keep the tab open. It will be a store for our test results. To perform tests, we will use vegeta. It's a small tool written in `Go` that can be used to measure site performance.

We need to create a job definition:

```
cat <<EOF |  curl -X POST -H "Content-Type: application/json" -d @
localhost:9000/v1/jobs/
{
  "description": "Mesos Agent /state performance test",
  "id": "vegeta",
  "run": {
    "artifacts": [{
      "uri":
"https://github.com/tsenart/vegeta/releases/download/v6.1.1/vegeta-v6.1.1-l
inux-amd64.tar.gz",
    }],
    "cmd": "echo 'GET http://localhost:5050/state' | ./vegeta -cpus 1
attack -duration=5s | ./vegeta -cpus 1 report --reporter json | curl -X
POST -d@- http://webhook.site/b105e9e3-7f5f-41db-b986-b837f6d5d319",
    "cpus": 1.0,
    "mem": 128,
    "disk": 0,
    "maxLaunchDelay": 60,
    "restart": {
      "policy": "NEVER"
    }
  }
}
EOF
```

Then we need to create a schedule for our run:

```
cat <<EOF |  curl -X POST -H "Content-Type: application/json" -d @-
localhost:9000/v1/jobs/vegeta/schedules
{
  "id": "at-every-5th-minute",
  "cron": "*/5 * * * *",
  "concurrencyPolicy": "ALLOW",
  "enabled": true,
  "startingDeadlineSeconds": 120,
  "timezone": "Etc/Zulu"
}
EOF
```

Now we can return to the browser and see the results of our tests:

Webhook.site with results of Metronome job

How it works...

Metronome, unlike Marathon, is designed to run one-off tasks. This means it runs tasks and expects them to finish with the status code 0. In the following example, we configured our job to download archives and run commands using one CPU and 128 MB of RAM. The disk limit set to 0 means that we didn't allocate a disk. For time-based job timing, it is very important. We can define what should happen if tasks don't start on time, or how and if they should be restarted. The max launch delay defines how much time a job has to start. If this timeout expires, it is aborted. The restart policy defines how to handle job failures. In our case, we didn't want to start another job if the first one failed.

After defining a job, we can create a schedule for it. One job can have more than one schedule. We use a `cron` expression to define when a job should be started. `startingDeadlineSeconds` defines how many seconds a job has to start before it is pointless and should be aborted.

Metronome supports Docker images as well. To run Docker, just add `"docker":{"image":"<your/image>"}` in the run section.

The Metronome API is small and well documented. Documentation can be found at `https://dcos.github.io/metronome/docs/generated/api.html#`.

8

Continuous Integration with Jenkins

In this chapter, you will learn how to install and configure Jenkins to use Mesos resources and run Jenkins jobs. This reduces infrastructure costs, since the same Mesos cluster could be used for Jenkins and other frameworks. Jenkins can scale dynamically, so developers aren't waiting for their builds. A pipeline introduced in Jenkins 2.0 and PaaS solutions such as Marathon allow you to build a whole system, taking care of building, testing and deployment. We will cover the following recipes in this chapter:

- Building the Jenkins Mesos plugin
- Configuring and running Jenkins jobs
- Running Jenkins jobs in Docker

Introduction

Jenkins is a well-known automation system. It is written in Java as a fork of Hudson (an automation system created by Sun Microsystems). Jenkins is designed to automate continuous integration and continuous deployment. It supports many code repositories with different triggers and build targets. It can be extended with plugins. The biggest advantage of Jenkins over other tools is its ability to run jobs on Mesos, which can reduce costs by reusing idle servers or easily spawning new build agents.

Building the Jenkins Mesos plugin

By default, Jenkins uses statically created agents and runs jobs on them. We can extend this behavior with a plugin that will make Jenkins use Mesos as a resource manager. Jenkins will register as a Mesos framework and accept offers when it needs to run a job.

Getting ready

You need to have Mesos up and running. See `Chapter 1`, *Getting Started with Apache Mesos* for more information.

How to do it...

The Jenkins Mesos plugin installation is a bit harder than Marathon. There are no official binary packages for it so it must be installed from sources:

1. First, we need to download the source code:

```
curl -L
https://github.com/jenkinsci/mesos-plugin/archive/mesos-0.14.0.tar.
gz | tar -zx
cd jenkinsci-mesos-plugin-*
```

2. The plugin is written in Java and to build it we need Maven (`mvn`):

```
sudo apt install maven
```

3. Finally, build the package:

```
mvn package
```

If everything goes smoothly, you should see information, that all tests passed and the plugin package will be placed in `target/mesos.hpi`.

How it works...

Jenkins is written in Java and presents an API for creating plugins. Plugins do not have to be written in Java, but must be compatible with those interfaces so most plugins are written in Java. The natural choice for building a Java application is Maven, although Gradle is getting more and more popular. The Jenkins Mesos plugin uses the Mesos native library to communicate with Mesos. This communication is now deprecated so the plugin does not support all Mesos features that are available with the Mesos HTTP API.

Installing Jenkins

We will be using Jenkins 2.32.1. Please be aware that future versions of Jenkins may require different steps if the screen changes. You can skip this recipe if you already have a running Jenkins installation.

How to do it...

1. Installing Jenkins is pretty straightforward. First, we need to add the Jenkins repository and it's key to the package sources of our system. After refreshing the packages list, we should be able to install Jenkins:

```
wget -q -O - https://pkg.jenkins.io/debian/jenkins-ci.org.key |
sudo apt-key add -
sudo sh -c 'echo deb http://pkg.jenkins.io/debian-stable binary/ >
/etc/apt/sources.list.d/jenkins.list'
sudo apt-get update
sudo apt-get install jenkins
```

2. By default, Jenkins will run on port 8080 and it should be running and waiting for configuration.
3. To change the default port, open /etc/default/Jenkins, find the following lines, and change the port and restart service:

```
# port for HTTP connector (default 8080; disable with -1)
HTTP_PORT=8080
```

4. At this point, Jenkins should be up and running and waiting for configuration. After opening a browser and pointing it to the Jenkins URL (for example, `10.10.10.10:8080`), it should look as follows:

5. To unlock Jenkins, follow the instructions and enter the password. Next, install the suggested plugins. There is a very good chance you will need them. If not, you can always remove unused plugins:

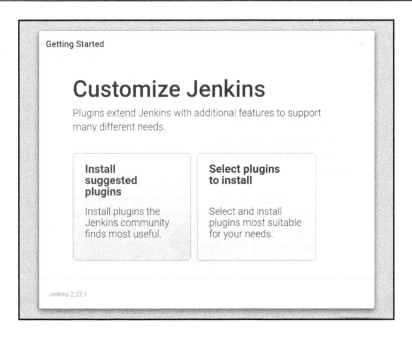

6. You can create a new user or continue as an admin. A user can be added later and configured with LDAP or another authentication provider used in your company, so continue as an admin:

7. Finally, you should be able to see the Jenkins dashboard. It should be empty because there are no jobs configured:

Enabling the Jenkins Mesos plugin

In this recipe, you will learn how to enable the Mesos Jenkins plugin and configure a job to be run on Mesos.

Getting ready

We assume you have built the Mesos Jenkins plugin. You will also need the Mesos cluster.

How to do it...

1. The first step is to install the Mesos Jenkins plugin. To do so, navigate to the Plugin Manager by clicking **Manage Jenkins** | **Manage Plugins**, and select the **Advanced tab**. You should see the following screen:

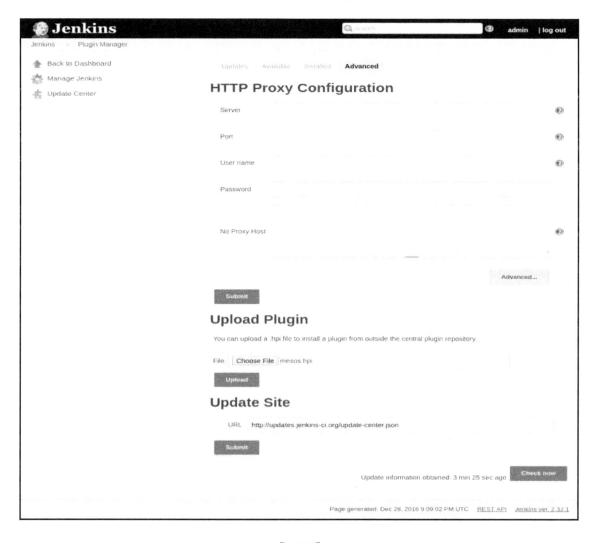

2. Click **Choose file** and select the previously built plugin to upload it. Once the plugin is installed, you have to configure it. To do so, go to the configuration (**Manage Jenkins** | **Configure System**). At the bottom of the page, the cloud section should appear. Fill in all the fields with the desired configuration values:

3. If you now disable **Advanced On- demand framework registration**, you should see the Jenkins Scheduler registered in the Mesos frameworks.

Remember to configure `Slave username` to the existing system user on Mesos agents. It will be used to run your jobs. By default, it will be `jenkins`. You can create it on slaves with the following command:

`adduser jenkins`

4. Be careful when providing an IP or hostnames for Mesos and Jenkins. It must match the IP used later by the scheduler for communication. By default, the Mesos native library binds to the interface that the hostname resolves to. This could lead to problems in communication, especially when receiving messages from Mesos. If you see your Jenkins is connected but jobs are stuck and agents do not start, check if Jenkins is registered with the proper IP. You can set the IP used by Jenkins by adding the following line in `/etc/default/jenkins` (in this example, we assume Jenkins should bind on `10.10.10.10`):

`LIBPROCESS IP=10.10.10.10`

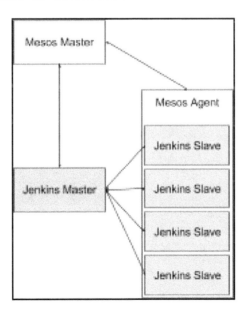

Index